GHOSTS

Henrik Ibsen
translated and adapted by
Anthony Clarvoe

BROADWAY PLAY PUBLISHING INC
New York
www.broadwayplaypublishing.com
info@broadwayplaypublishing.com

GHOSTS

© Copyright 2016 by Anthony Clarvoe

Cover image: Edvard Munch set design

I S B N: 978-0-88145-656-1

First printing: April 2016

Book design: Marie Donovan
Page make-up: Adobe Indesign
Typeface: Palatino

This version of GHOSTS was commissioned by Cincinnati Playhouse in the Park and the Repertory Theater of St Louis.

GHOSTS was produced by Cincinnati Playhouse in the Park (Ed Stern, Producing Artistic Director; Buzz Ward, Executive Director), opening on 20 February, 1996. The cast and creative contributors were:

MRS HELENA ALVING................................Maeve Mcguire
OSWALD ALVING...................................Timothy Altmeyer
PASTOR MANDERS............................ William Whitehead
JACOB ENGSTRAND...James Doerr
REGINA ENGSTRAND .... Penny Balfour

Director...Madeleine Pabis
Set ....Marie Anne Chiment
Costumes...Barbra Kravitz
Lighting...Jackie Manassee
Sound .... David B Smith
Stage manager...Jenifer Morrow

GHOSTS was subsequently produced by the Repertory Theater of St Louis (Steven Woolf, Artistic Director; Mark D Bernstein, Managing Director), opening on 20 March 1996. The cast and creative contributors were:

MRS HELENA ALVING .... Peggy Friesen
OSWALD ALVING .... Matthew Rauch
PASTOR MANDERS .... Joneal Joplin
JACOB ENGSTRAND .... Robert Elliott
REGINA ENGSTRAND .... Pilar Witherspoon

Director .... John Dillon
Set & costumes .... Lindsay W Davis
Lighting .... Max De Volder
Stage manager .... Champe Leary

GHOSTS was then produced by Intiman Theatre (Warner Shook, Artistic Director; Laura Penn, Managing Director), opening on 23 October 1996. The cast and creative contributors were:

MRS HELENA ALVING .... Barbara Dirickson
OSWALD ALVING .... Henri Lubatti
PASTOR MANDERS .... Daniel Mooney
JACOB ENGSTRAND .... Kurt Beattie
REGINA ENGSTRAND .... Libby Christophersen

Director .... Richard E T White
Set .... Karen Gjelsteen
Costumes .... Rose Pederson
Lighting .... Rick Paulsen
Composer/sound .... Jim Ragland
Dramaturg .... Denise Koschmann
Stage manager .... Tamara Schlief

A NOTE FROM THE TRANSLATOR/ ADAPTOR

The distinction the theater makes between new plays and revivals is misleading. The only reason to revive a play, and the only way truly to do it, is to create a new event. In GHOSTS, a woman has to face her legacy of religious and sexual repression when her grown son comes home to tell her he has an incurable sexually-transmitted disease and to ask her to help him die with dignity. Without moving an inch from his provincial Norway, Ibsen's play is about and for our time.

There is, of course, a distance for his collaborators to travel. Today's theater artists have a prurience about dramatic manipulation almost as reflexive as the Victorians' about sex: we know we couldn't exist without it, but we're appalled when we see it happening. In Ibsen's day, audiences were horror-struck at his sexual frankness; in the century since, many theater artists have been shocked by how blatantly he seduces an audience with the rude push and pull of melodrama. Ibsen designed his work for maximum impact onstage: he writes magnificently meaty acting parts, gets his laughs, raises the stakes of his characters' encounters, tightens his suspense, sets his explosions, springs his twists of plot, buttons his scenes, writes outrageous curtain lines.

So why has Ibsen developed a reputation in this
country as something of an eat-your-spinach literary
figure? In a word: translation.

Norwegian is not very difficult to translate into a kind
of English. The many old cognates and common roots
render a kind of Middle English prosody. The next
step is a greater challenge. Most available translations
of Ibsen into English have been written either by
playwrights who have never seen his Norwegian and
are cribbing from someone else's "literal" translation,
or by translators fluent in Norwegian who have never
seen a rehearsal room. The playwrights miss Ibsen's
specific idioms, whose imagery resonates through the
play. The translators lose his rhythmic propulsion:
each of their lines is a syllable or two longer than the
original, resulting in a talkiness for which Ibsen takes
the blame. His works are usually divided into the verse
plays and the plays in prose. Most Ibsen translations
are just that: prose.

But Ibsen did not write prose. He wrote stage dialogue,
speaking language, flung with snap and tension from
actor to actor, as the players rally the shuttlecock
of ceaseless concentration into an almost palpable
webwork of energy. In stage dialogue, even the pauses
pulse with momentum. This net of energy can be
an end in itself; the game is grand fun. In the great
playwrights, it can also be the springboard for ideas,
creating a dialectics in action. It can be the rigging we
climb to catharsis, the hardest height of theater.

Working on these productions and those of other
translations since has forced me to learn that a vital
part of the translator's work is to render not simply
the meaning of each word or each line, but of the play
as a whole, as best I understand it. For a production
script that can sometimes mean cutting a line, or a
beat, or adding (with excruciating care) a word or

two to help a contemporary audience and a play from another time and place find a larger common ground of understanding. For my ongoing education in this work I am grateful to all the artists listed above, the audiences who watched them, and many more in the years that have followed.

That said, the language here is Ibsen's, in English as taut as I can turn it. Most translators' Norwegian is more fluent than mine, as the thumb-blackened edges of my grammars and dictionaries will attest. What I hope this GHOSTS has to offer is the language of theater: charged dialogue for the American stage.

CHARACTERS & SETTING

MRS HELENA ALVING, *widow of a captain and chamberlain*
OSWALD ALVING, *her son, a painter*
PASTOR MANDERS
ENGSTRAND, *a carpenter*
REGINA ENGSTRAND, MRS ALVING's *housemaid*

Setting: MRS ALVING's *estate, on a large fjord in western Norway*

ACT ONE

(*A spacious conservatory with a door on the left wall and
two doors on the wall to the right. In the middle of the room
is a round table with chairs around it; on the table lie bottles,
magazines, and newspapers. In the foreground to the left is
a window, and by it a little sofa with a sewing table in front
of it. In the background the room continues into a somewhat
smaller greenhouse, enclosed by large panes of glass. On
the greenhouse's right wall is a door, which leads down to
the garden. Through the glass walls shows a gloomy fjord-
landscape, veiled by a steady rain.*)

(ENGSTRAND, *a carpenter, stands in the garden door. His
left leg is somewhat crooked; he has a block of wood under his
bootsole.* REGINA, *with an empty watering can in her hand,
blocks his path.*)

REGINA: (*In a muffled voice*) What do you want? Stay
where you are. You're dripping.

ENGSTRAND: That's the Lord's own rain, my child.

REGINA: Rain from hell is what it is.

ENGSTRAND: Lord, the way you talk, Regina. (*Limps
a few steps forward into the room*) But what I wanted to
say—

REGINA: And stop clomping around with that foot! The
young gentleman's asleep upstairs.

ENGSTRAND: He's still asleep? In broad daylight?

REGINA: That's none of your business.

ENGSTRAND: I was out last night myself—

REGINA: That I can believe.

ENGSTRAND: Yes, for we mortals are weak, my child—

REGINA: Aren't we though.

ENGSTRAND: —and manifold are the temptations of this world, y'know—but even so, there I was, yes by God, at my work by half past five this morning.

REGINA: All right, all right, now come on. I won't stand here and have a *rendez-vous* with you.

ENGSTRAND: You won't have a what?

REGINA: I won't have anyone find you here. So. On your way.

ENGSTRAND: *(Draws a couple of steps nearer)* Hell if I'll go before I have a talk with you. This afternoon I finish the work down there on the schoolhouse, then tonight I head home to town on the steamboat.

REGINA: *(Muttering)* Happy sailing!

ENGSTRAND: Thank you, my child. Tomorrow when they dedicate the Orphanage they'll probably be carrying on up here, y'know, with intoxicating drink. And nobody's going to say that Jacob Engstrand can't hold his own when temptation comes along.

REGINA: Ha!

ENGSTRAND: Because a lot of the finer type of people will be here. Parson Manders, too, he's expected from town.

REGINA: He's coming today.

ENGSTRAND: There, you see? And I'm damned if he's going to get anything on me, you judge for yourself.

REGINA: Aha, so that's it!

ENGSTRAND: What's it?

REGINA: What are you going to con Parson Manders out of this time?

ENGSTRAND: Sh, sh; what's the matter with you? Would I con Parson Manders out of anything? Oh no, Parson Manders has been much too kind to me for that. But here's what I wanted to talk with you about, y'know: tonight I finally leave for home.

REGINA: The sooner you leave the better for me.

ENGSTRAND: Yes, but I want you with me, Regina.

REGINA: *(Open-mouthed)* You want me—? What are you saying?

ENGSTRAND: I'm saying I want you home with me.

REGINA: *(Scornfully)* Never in eternity will you get me home with you.

ENGSTRAND: Well, we'll see about that.

REGINA: Oh, we'll see about it. When I've been raised in the Chamberlain's house? —When Mrs Alving's treated me almost like her child?—I should come home to you? To a house like that? Pff!

ENGSTRAND: What the hell is this? Standing up to your father, Miss?

REGINA: *(Mumbling, without looking at him)* You've often said I was none of your doing.

ENGSTRAND: Pah; what do you want to bring that up for—

REGINA: Haven't you—how many times—

ENGSTRAND: By God, I have never said a word—

REGINA: Oh, I remember the word you used.

ENGSTRAND: But that was only when I was, you know, on edge—hm. Manifold are the temptations of this world, Regina.

REGINA: Ugh!

ENGSTRAND: And when your mother would turn on me—I had to find something to give her hell about, my child. She always had to be so fine. *(Mimics)* "Let me go, Engstrand! Let me be! I served for three years on Chamberlain Alving's estate—!" *(Laughs)* Lord save us; she never could forget the Captain became Chamberlain while she worked here.

REGINA: Poor mother—you tortured her life away soon enough.

ENGSTRAND: *(With a bow)* Oh, that's understood: I'm to blame for everything.

REGINA: *(Turning away, under her breath)* And that leg.

ENGSTRAND: What did you say, my child?

REGINA: *Pied de mouton.*

ENGSTRAND: What is that, German?

REGINA: Yes.

ENGSTRAND: Well well, you've gotten some learning out here, and that'll do you some good now, Regina.

REGINA: *(After a short pause)* So what did you want with me in town?

ENGSTRAND: Can you ask what a father wants with his own child? Aren't I a solitary and forsaken widower?

REGINA: Oh, don't try that on me. Why do you want me down there?

ENGSTRAND: I'll tell you. I've been thinking of starting on something new.

REGINA: *(Snorting)* Again? It always goes wrong.

ENGSTRAND: But this time, just you watch, Regina!—
Hell, if I don't—

REGINA: *(Stamping her foot)* Stop swearing!

ENGSTRAND: Sh, sh; you're ever so right, my child! I
just wanted to say—I've put away a little money from
the work on this new Orphanage.

REGINA: Have you? Good for you.

ENGSTRAND: What else can a man do with his spare
change, out here in the country?

REGINA: So?

ENGSTRAND: So, y'know, I'd thought I'd put the money
into something that could pay. It could be a sort of an
inn, for sailors—

REGINA: Ee-yuh!

ENGSTRAND: A really fine inn, you judge for yourself—
not some pigsty for deck hands. No, damn it, it would
be for captains and first mates and—and the finer type
of people, you judge for yourself.

REGINA: And I would—?

ENGSTRAND: You get to help, right? Just for the look of
things, you understand. You wouldn't have a damn
bit of work to do, my child. You can do whatever you
want.

REGINA: Uh huh!

ENGSTRAND: But there've got to be women in the
house, that's plain as day. Because in the evenings
we'll want a little entertainment, singing and dancing
and so on. You have to remember these are sailors,
wayfarers on the oceans of the world. *(Approaching
her)* Now don't be stupid and stand in your own way,
Regina. What are you going to do out here? What good
is this learning the lady's been feeding you? I hear

you'll be nursing the orphans. What's in that for you? Are you really so hungry to wear yourself out for the sake of some grubby brats?

REGINA: No, if things go the way I want, then—Well, we'll see. We'll see!

ENGSTRAND: What do you mean, what'll we see?

REGINA: Don't you worry about that. How much money have you put away up here?

ENGSTRAND: All in all, it comes to a good seven, eight hundred crowns.

REGINA: That's not bad.

ENGSTRAND: It's enough to get started with, my child.

REGINA: Don't you think you should give me some of that money?

ENGSTRAND: God no, I don't think that, no.

REGINA: Don't you think you should send me a big enough rag to make a dress with for once?

ENGSTRAND: In town with me, you can get all the dresses you want.

REGINA: Pah, I can get my hands on them on my own, if I want to.

ENGSTRAND: No, a father's guiding hand is better, Regina. Now I can get a nice house in Little Harbor Street. It won't take a lot of cash; and it could become a sort of sailors' home, y'know.

REGINA: But I don't wish to live with you! I've got nothing to do with you. So go!

ENGSTRAND: You wouldn't stay with me so damn long, my child. Not likely! If you know how to behave. As pretty a miss as you've become in the last year—

REGINA: Well—?

ENGSTRAND: It won't be long before some first mate comes along—yes, maybe a captain—

REGINA: I don't want to marry someone like that. Sailors have got no *savoir vivre*.

ENGSTRAND: They've got no what?

REGINA: I'm saying I know about sailors. They're no one to get married to.

ENGSTRAND: So don't marry them. That can pay just as well. *(More confidentially)* He—the Englishman—the one with the pleasure-boat—he gave three hundred crowns—and she was no prettier than you.

REGINA: *(Going after him)* You get out!

ENGSTRAND: *(Backing away)* Now, now, you don't want to hit me.

REGINA: Yes! Say one word about Mother and I will hit you. I'm telling you, get out! *(Driving him up towards the garden door)* And don't slam the doors; young Mr. Alving—

ENGSTRAND: He's sleeping, yes. You make a lot of fuss over young Mister Alving— *(Staring)* Hoho; it couldn't be by any chance that he—?

REGINA: Out, and fast! You're out of your mind! No, not that way. Here comes Pastor Manders. Down the kitchen stairs, go.

ENGSTRAND: *(Towards the right)* All right, I'll go. But talk with him, when he gets here. He's the man to tell you what a child owes her father. Because after all, I am your father, y'know. I can prove it by the parish register.

(ENGSTRAND *goes out through the second door, as* REGINA *opens and then locks it after him. She hastily looks at herself in the mirror, dusts herself with her pocket handkerchief and straightens her collar; then she busies herself with the flowers.)*

(PASTOR MANDERS, in an overcoat and with an umbrella, along with a little traveling-bag over his shoulder, comes through the garden door into the greenhouse.)

PASTOR MANDERS: Good day, Miss Engstrand.

REGINA: *(Turning, in happy surprise)* Oh, good day, Pastor! Has the steamboat come in already?

PASTOR MANDERS: It came in just now. *(Going into the sitting-room)* What tedious weather we're having, rain every day.

REGINA: *(Following him)* It's such blessed weather for the farmers, Pastor.

PASTOR MANDERS: Yes, you're quite right there. We townspeople think so little about that. *(He starts taking off his overcoat.)*

REGINA: Oh, can't I help you? There. Oh, it's so wet! I'll just hang it up in the hallway. And your umbrella—I'll open it up, so it can dry out.

(REGINA goes out with the things through the second door on the right. PASTOR MANDERS takes off his traveling-bag and lays it and his hat on a chair. Meanwhile REGINA comes in again.)

PASTOR MANDERS: Oh, it feels so good to get indoors. So, is everything still going well here?

REGINA: Yes, many thanks.

PASTOR MANDERS: Keeping busy, I would imagine, getting ready for tomorrow?

REGINA: Oh yes, there's a great deal to do here.

PASTOR MANDERS: And Mrs Alving, I hope, is at home?

REGINA: Of course; she's just upstairs, taking the young gentleman some hot chocolate.

PASTOR MANDERS: Yes, tell me—I heard down at the dock that Oswald had come.

REGINA: Yes, the day before yesterday. We didn't expect him till today.

PASTOR MANDERS: Hale and hearty, I hope?

REGINA: Yes, thanks, that he is. But terribly tired from the journey. He took the train straight from Paris—I mean, he came all this way without stopping once. I think he's sleeping a little now, so we should talk a bit softly.

PASTOR MANDERS: Sh, we'll be quiet then.

REGINA: *(As she moves an armchair next to the table)* Please sit down, Pastor, make yourself comfortable. *(As he sits, she moves a footstool under his feet)* So! Are you comfortable now, Pastor?

PASTOR MANDERS: Thanks, thanks; this is excellent. *(Looking at her)* Listen, do you know, Miss Engstrand, I do believe you have grown up since I saw you last.

REGINA: Do you think so, Pastor? Mrs Alving says I've filled out, too.

PASTOR MANDERS: Filled out? Well yes, perhaps, a little; quite passably.

(A short pause)

REGINA: Should I call Mrs Alving?

PASTOR MANDERS: Thanks, thanks, there's no hurry, my dear child. Well now, tell me, Regina, how is your father doing out here?

REGINA: Oh, thanks, Pastor, he's getting along pretty well.

PASTOR MANDERS: He came by my place the last time he was in town.

REGINA: Did he? He's always so glad to talk with you, Pastor.

PASTOR MANDERS: And you, I assume, look in on him faithfully every day?

REGINA: Me? Oh, often enough; when I have the time—

PASTOR MANDERS: Your father does not have a very strong character, Miss Engstrand. He needs a guiding hand.

REGINA: Oh, I can believe that.

PASTOR MANDERS: He needs someone with him, someone he is fond of, and whose judgment he can give weight to. He admitted it himself, quite openly, when he came to see me.

REGINA: Yes, he's talked like that to me, too. But I don't know if Mrs Alving can do without me—especially now that we have the new Orphanage to run. And I'd be terribly unhappy to leave Mrs Alving, too, she's always been so kind to me.

PASTOR MANDERS: But a daughter's duty, my good girl—Naturally we would have to get your mistress's permission.

REGINA: But I don't know that it would be right for me, at my age, to keep house for a single man.

PASTOR MANDERS: What! My dear Miss Engstrand, this is your own father we're talking about!

REGINA: Maybe so, but still—Oh, if it were in a good house, with a real gentleman—

PASTOR MANDERS: But, my dear Regina—

REGINA: —someone I could feel devoted to and look up to and be like a daughter to—

PASTOR MANDERS: Yes, but my dear, good child—

REGINA: Because then I would be happy to go to town. It's very lonely out here—and the Pastor knows himself what it means to be alone in the world. And believe me, I'm willing and able. Doesn't the Pastor know of a place like that for me?

PASTOR MANDERS: Me? No, I absolutely don't.

REGINA: My dear, dear, Pastor—think of me anyway, if—

PASTOR MANDERS: *(Rising)* Yes, I'll do that, Miss Engstrand.

REGINA: Because if I—

PASTOR MANDERS: Would you, perhaps, be so good as to call your mistress?

REGINA: She'll come right away, Pastor.

(REGINA goes out the left door. PASTOR MANDERS paces a couple of times up and down the room, stands a moment with his hands behind his back, and looks out at the garden. Then he comes near the table again, takes a book and looks at the title-page, starts, and looks at several of them.)

PASTOR MANDERS: Hm—well now!

(MRS ALVING enters through the door on the left. She is followed by REGINA, who goes straight out the first door on the right.)

MRS ALVING: *(Giving him her hand)* Welcome, Pastor.

PASTOR MANDERS: Good day, ma'am. Here I am, as promised.

MRS ALVING: Always so punctual.

PASTOR MANDERS: Believe you me, it took some doing to get away. All those blessed commissions and committees—

MRS ALVING: All the kinder of you to come so early. Now we can get our business settled before lunch. But where is your luggage?

PASTOR MANDERS: *(Quickly)* My things are down at the village. I'll stay there tonight.

MRS ALVING: *(Suppressing a smile)* I really can't persuade you to stay overnight in my house, even now?

PASTOR MANDERS: No, no, ma'am; many thanks all the same; I'll stay down there, as usual. It's so convenient to the steamboat.

MRS ALVING: As you wish. But all the same I would think that two old people like us—

PASTOR MANDERS: Oh, God preserve me from your teasing. Well, you must be overjoyed today. First the celebration tomorrow, and you've got your Oswald home.

MRS ALVING: Yes, can you imagine how happy I am! It's two years since he was home last. And he's promised to stay with me all winter long.

PASTOR MANDERS: Has he? That's splendid, that's what a son should be. For there must be very different attractions to life in Rome or Paris, I would think.

MRS ALVING: Yes, but here at home he has his mother, you know. Ah, my blessed boy—he still has room in his heart for his mother!

PASTOR MANDERS: It would surely be too sad, if absence and preoccupation with such a thing as art should blunt his natural feelings.

MRS ALVING: Yes, indeed. But, there's no trouble like that with him, no. Well, I'll enjoy seeing if you recognize him. He'll come down soon; he's lying upstairs just now, resting a little on the sofa. But sit down, my dear Pastor.

PASTOR MANDERS: Thanks. You are quite free to—?

MRS ALVING: Of course. *(She sits by the table.)*

PASTOR MANDERS: Good; then you shall see— *(He goes to the chair where his traveling-bag lies, takes a packet of papers out of it, sits down at the opposite side of the table and looks for a clear place for the papers.)* Now here we have, first— *(Breaking off)* Tell me, Mrs Alving, how did these books come to be here?

MRS ALVING: These books? These are books I'm reading.

PASTOR MANDERS: You read this sort of writing?

MRS ALVING: I certainly do.

PASTOR MANDERS: Do you feel that you are made better or happier by this sort of reading?

MRS ALVING: I feel that I have become a little more secure.

PASTOR MANDERS: That is remarkable. How is that?

MRS ALVING: I find they're a kind of evidence, a confirmation of many things I've come to think myself. Yes, because what is strange, Pastor Manders—there's nothing really new in these books; nothing but what most people think and believe. It's just that most people either can't make sense of it for themselves or they don't want to have it around.

PASTOR MANDERS: But my God, you seriously believe that most people—?

MRS ALVING: Of course I believe it.

PASTOR MANDERS: Yes, but, after all, not in this country? Not here?

MRS ALVING: Oh yes, here, too.

PASTOR MANDERS: Well, I must say—!

MRS ALVING: Besides, what exactly do you object to in these books?

PASTOR MANDERS: Object to? You surely don't believe that I spend my time studying publications like these?

MRS ALVING: Meaning you have no idea what you're condemning?

PASTOR MANDERS: I have read enough about these writings to disapprove of them.

MRS ALVING: Yes, but in your own opinion—

PASTOR MANDERS: Dear Madam, there are many times in this life when we must trust to others. That is how things are sometimes in this world; and that is good. Otherwise what would become of society?

MRS ALVING: You may be right there.

PASTOR MANDERS: By the way, I don't deny, of course, that there may be a great deal that is attractive in such writing. And I can hardly blame you for wanting to acquaint yourself with so-called intellectual trends in the outside world—where you have let your son make his way for so long. But—

MRS ALVING: But—

PASTOR MANDERS: (*Lowering his voice*) But one doesn't have to talk about it, Mrs Alving. One is surely not bound to account to everyone for what one reads and what one thinks within one's own four walls—

MRS ALVING: No, of course not.

PASTOR MANDERS: But consider your responsibility to this Orphanage, now, which you decided to build at a time when your feelings on spiritual matters were very different from what they are now -- so far as I can judge.

MRS ALVING: All right, I admit it. But it was about the Orphanage—

PASTOR MANDERS: It is about the Orphanage we should speak, yes. So then—discretion, dear Madam! And now we'll go on to our business. *(Opening the packet and taking out papers)* Do you see these?

MRS ALVING: The documents?

PASTOR MANDERS: All of them. Perfectly in order. Believe you me, it took some doing to get them in time. I really had to push. The authorities are almost painfully conscientious when it comes to making decisions. But here we have them at last. *(Leafing through the bundle)* The quitclaim deed for the Solvig estate, in the Rosenvold Manor, together with the newly constructed housing, schoolhall, teacher's residence and chapel. And the authorization for the endowment and by-laws for the foundation. You see— *(Reading)* By-laws for the Captain Alving Memorial Children's Home.

MRS ALVING: *(Looking a long time at the paper)* So there it is.

PASTOR MANDERS: I chose the title "Captain" instead of "Chamberlain." Captain seems less ostentatious.

MRS ALVING: All right, whatever you like.

PASTOR MANDERS: And here you have the account book for the endowment.

MRS ALVING: Thanks; but keep it please, for convenience's sake.

PASTOR MANDERS: Gladly. I think we'll let the money stay in the bank to start with. The interest certainly isn't very attractive; four percent with six months' notice of withdrawal. Later, if a good mortgage could be found—naturally it would have to be a first mortgage, with collateral of unquestionable security—then we might reconsider.

MRS ALVING: All right, dear Pastor Manders, whatever you judge best.

PASTOR MANDERS: In any case, I'll keep my eyes open. But there is one thing I've meant to ask you several times.

MRS ALVING: What is that?

PASTOR MANDERS: The endowment is sufficient to cover the ongoing expenses.

MRS ALVING: Yes.

PASTOR MANDERS: But what if, say, an accident were to happen? We can never know, of course—Would you be able to make good the damage?

MRS ALVING: No, I tell you outright, I would not do that at all.

PASTOR MANDERS: Well then. I suppose—we have to trust that an institution like this has luck with it—

MRS ALVING: Let's hope so, Pastor Manders.

PASTOR MANDERS: Yes, that it stands under a special protection—

MRS ALVING: It's strange that you happen to bring this up today—

PASTOR MANDERS: I've often meant to ask you about it—

MRS ALVING: -- because yesterday we nearly had a fire down there.

PASTOR MANDERS: What?

MRS ALVING: It was nothing, really. Some shavings caught fire in the carpenters' workshop.

PASTOR MANDERS: Where Engstrand works?

MRS ALVING: Yes. He's often careless with matches, they say.

PASTOR MANDERS: He has so many things on his mind, that man—so much standing in his way. Thank God, he's committed himself to leading a blameless life, so I hear.

MRS ALVING: Indeed? Who says that?

PASTOR MANDERS: He's assured me of it himself. And he's certainly a clever workman, too.

MRS ALVING: As long as he's sober—

PASTOR MANDERS: Yes, that tragic weakness! It's on account of his bad leg, he says. The last time he was in town, I truly was touched by him. He came up to me and thanked me so sincerely for getting him work here, so he could be near Regina.

MRS ALVING: He doesn't see very much of her.

PASTOR MANDERS: He talks with her every day, he told me so himself.

MRS ALVING: Yes, maybe so.

PASTOR MANDERS: He feels so keenly that he needs someone who can restrain him when temptation comes near. That is what's so lovable about Jacob Engstrand, he comes quite helplessly and accuses himself and confesses his weakness. The last time he spoke with me— Listen, Mrs Alving, if it is his heart's desire to have Regina home with him again—

MRS ALVING: (*Rising hastily*) Regina!

PASTOR MANDERS: —you mustn't stand in his way.

MRS ALVING: I certainly will stand in his way.
Besides—Regina will have a position at the Orphanage.

PASTOR MANDERS: But remember, after all, he is her
father—

MRS ALVING: I know very well what kind of father
he's been to her. No, she will never go to him with my
blessing.

PASTOR MANDERS: *(Rising)* But, dear Madam, please
don't take it so badly. It's sad, the way you misjudge
poor Engstrand. You seem almost frightened—

MRS ALVING: *(Quieter)* All the same. I have taken
Regina in here with me, and she will stay here with me.
(Listening) Hush, dear Pastor Manders, don't say any
more about it. *(Brightening)* Listen! Oswald is coming
downstairs. Now we'll think only of him.

(OSWALD ALVING, *in a light overcoat, with his hat in
his hand and smoking a large meerschaum pipe, comes in
through the door on the left.)*

OSWALD: *(Stopping in the doorway)* Oh, forgive me—I
thought you were in the study. *(Coming closer)* Good
day, Pastor.

PASTOR MANDERS: *(Staring)* Ah—! How strange—

MRS ALVING: Well, what do you think of him, Pastor
Manders?

PASTOR MANDERS: I think—I think—No, but is it
really—?

OSWALD: Yes, it really is, the Prodigal Son, Pastor.

PASTOR MANDERS: But my dear young friend—

OSWALD: Well, the son come home, then.

MRS ALVING: Oswald is thinking of the time when you
were so opposed to his becoming a painter.

PASTOR MANDERS: To the eyes of reason many a step may well seem doubtful, which afterwards though— *(Wringing his hand)* Welcome, welcome! No, my dear Oswald—May I still call you by your first name?

OSWALD: Yes, what else should you call me?

PASTOR MANDERS: Good. This is what I wanted to say, my dear Oswald. You mustn't think that I absolutely condemn the artist's trade. I expect there are many who can preserve the inner man uncorrupted even in that trade.

OSWALD: Let's hope so.

MRS ALVING: *(Beaming delightedly)* I know one who's kept both the inner and the outer man uncorrupted. Just look at him, Pastor Manders.

OSWALD: *(Moving up the floor)* All right, Mother dear, let it go.

PASTOR MANDERS: Absolutely—that's indisputable. And you've already started to make a name for yourself. The newspapers often talk about you, and very favorably. Well, it would seem—lately it seems to me they've been a bit quieter.

OSWALD: *(Up in the greenhouse)* I haven't gotten to paint so much lately.

MRS ALVING: Even a painter has to rest sometimes.

PASTOR MANDERS: I should think so. And prepare himself and gird his strength for something great.

OSWALD: Yes. Mother, will we eat soon?

MRS ALVING: In less than half an hour. He certainly has an appetite, thank God.

PASTOR MANDERS: And a taste for tobacco, as well.

OSWALD: I found father's pipe upstairs in the bedroom and—

PASTOR MANDERS: Ah, that's it!

MRS ALVING: What?

PASTOR MANDERS: When Oswald came in the door with the pipe in his mouth, I thought I saw his father in the flesh.

OSWALD: Really?

MRS ALVING: Oh, how can you say that? Oswald takes after me.

PASTOR MANDERS: Yes; but there is an expression at the corners of his mouth, something about the lips, that reminds me exactly of Alving—in any case, now that he's smoking.

MRS ALVING: Not in the least. Oswald has something rather ministerial about the mouth, it seems to me.

PASTOR MANDERS: Oh yes, oh yes; several of my colleagues have a similar expression.

MRS ALVING: But put the pipe away, my dear; I won't have smoking in here.

OSWALD: *(Doing so)* Gladly. I only wanted to try it because I smoked it once when I was a boy.

MRS ALVING: You?

OSWALD: I was very little at the time. And as I remember, one evening he was in such a good mood that I went up to Father's bedroom.

MRS ALVING: You don't remember a thing from those years.

OSWALD: I remember it clearly, he took and sat me on his knee and let me smoke his pipe. Smoke, boy, he said, smoke away, boy! And I smoked as hard as I could, until I began to feel faint, and big drops of sweat broke out on my forehead. He burst out laughing—

PASTOR MANDERS: That's very strange.

MRS ALVING: My dear, it's only something Oswald dreamed.

OSWALD: No, Mother, it wasn't a dream at all. Don't you remember—you came in and carried me off to the nursery. I was sick all over and I saw that you were crying. Did father play tricks like that a lot?

PASTOR MANDERS: He was quite a spirited young man—

OSWALD: Anyway, he did accomplish so much in the world. So much that was good and useful, even though he died so young.

PASTOR MANDERS: Yes, you truly have received an active and worthy man's name as your legacy, my dear Oswald Alving. Well, let us hopeful it will be a spur to you—

OSWALD: It should be, yes.

PASTOR MANDERS: It was splendid of you in any case to come home for the ceremony in his honor.

OSWALD: It's the least I could do for Father.

MRS ALVING: And I get to keep him so long—that's even more splendid.

PASTOR MANDERS: Yes, you'll be home all winter long, I hear.

OSWALD: I'll be home for an indefinite time, Pastor. Oh, it really is lovely to come home!

MRS ALVING: *(Beaming)* Yes, truly, isn't it good?

PASTOR MANDERS: *(Looking sympathetically at him)* You went out early into the world, my dear Oswald.

OSWALD: That I did. Sometimes I wonder if it wasn't too early.

MRS ALVING: Oh, not at all. It's just as well for a healthy boy. Especially an only son. He shouldn't stay home with his mother and father, getting spoiled.

PASTOR MANDERS: That's a highly debatable question, Mrs Alving. His parents' home is and always will be a child's proper place.

OSWALD: I have to agree with the Pastor there.

PASTOR MANDERS: Just look, now, at your own son. Yes, we may just as well speak of it in his presence. What has been the upshot for him? He is twenty-six or -seven years old and he's never had a chance to get to know a decent home.

OSWALD: Forgive me, Pastor—there you are mistaken.

PASTOR MANDERS: Indeed? I thought you had traveled almost exclusively in artistic circles.

OSWALD: So I have.

PASTOR MANDERS: And mainly among the younger artists.

OSWALD: Yes, of course.

PASTOR MANDERS: But I thought that most of those people couldn't afford to support a family and maintain a home.

OSWALD: Many of them can't afford to get married, Pastor.

PASTOR MANDERS: Yes, that is just what I mean.

OSWALD: But they may well have a home all the same. And so they have, some of them, very decent, very comfortable homes.

(MRS ALVING *follows closely, nodding but saying nothing.*)

PASTOR MANDERS: But I am not talking about bachelors' homes. By a home I mean a family home, where a husband lives with his wife and children.

OSWALD: Yes; or where a man and a woman live together, with their children.

PASTOR MANDERS: *(Starting; clasping his hands)* But merciful God—!

OSWALD: Well?

PASTOR MANDERS: They openly live together—in front of children!

OSWALD: Yes, would you rather they got rid of them somehow?

PASTOR MANDERS: So you're talking about unmarried couples! About these so-called common-law marriages!

OSWALD: I've never noticed anything particularly common about these people's lives together.

PASTOR MANDERS: But how is it possible that a—a reasonably well brought-up man or young woman can bear to live like that—in front of everyone!

OSWALD: But what should they do? A poor young artist, a poor young girl—It costs a lot of money to get married. What should they do?

PASTOR MANDERS: What should they do? Well, Mister Alving, I'll tell you what they should do. They should keep off each other in the first place, that's what they should do!

OSWALD: Your speech won't get you far with young, warm-blooded people in love.

MRS ALVING: No, it won't get you far.

PASTOR MANDERS: And that the authorities tolerate such things! That they permit them to take place openly! *(Turning to MRS ALVING)* Didn't I have good reason to be deeply concerned for your son? In circles where open immorality can hold sway and even seems to be insisted upon—

OSWALD: I'll tell you something, Pastor. I've been a regular Sunday guest in a couple of such immoral homes—

PASTOR MANDERS: And on Sunday, yet!

OSWALD: Yes, isn't it the day to enjoy ourselves? But never have I heard an offensive word, much less been witness to anything that could be called immoral. No; do you know when and where I've come across immorality in artistic circles?

PASTOR MANDERS: No, God be thanked!

OSWALD: Then I'll take the liberty to tell you. I've come across it when one or another of our model husbands and family men has come down to take a little look for himself—and has done the artists the honor to drop into their humble cafs. Then we'd get the message. These gentlemen could tell us about places and things we'd never dreamed of.

PASTOR MANDERS: What? Do you mean that honorable men from our home here would—?

OSWALD: Haven't you ever, when such honorable men come home again, haven't you ever heard them speak out against the rampant immorality abroad?

PASTOR MANDERS: Well, naturally—

MRS ALVING: I've heard them as well.

OSWALD: Well, you can take their word for it. There are experts among them. (Holding his head) Oh—the beautiful, glorious freedom of life out there—why do they have to make it obscene.

MRS ALVING: You mustn't overexcite yourself, Oswald; it isn't good for you.

OSWALD: No, you're right, mother. It probably isn't
healthy for me. It's the damned tiredness, you see.
Well, I'll go for a little walk before lunch. Forgive me,
Pastor; you can't understand; that's just the way it
strikes me. *(He goes out through the second door to the
right.)*

MRS ALVING: My poor boy—!

PASTOR MANDERS: You may well say so. So this is what
he has come to!

(MRS ALVING looks at him silently.)

PASTOR MANDERS: *(Walking up and down)* He called
himself the Prodigal Son—And what do you say to all
this?

MRS ALVING: I say that Oswald was right in every
word.

PASTOR MANDERS: *(Standing still)* Right? Right? In such
principles?

MRS ALVING: Here in my solitude I've come to the
same way of thinking, Pastor. But I've never dared to
speak up. Well and good, now my boy will speak for
me.

PASTOR MANDERS: I feel such sorrow for you, Mrs
Alving. I want to have a serious word with you. Not as
your business manager and adviser, not as your and
your husband's childhood friend, but as the priest who
stood before you like this in the moment of your life
when you were most lost.

MRS ALVING: And what does my priest have to say to
me?

PASTOR MANDERS: First I want to stir your memory,
ma'am. The time is right. Tomorrow is the tenth
anniversary of your husband's death. Tomorrow the
memorial in his honor will be unveiled. Tomorrow I'll

speak to the crowd that will gather here—but today I want to speak to you alone.

MRS ALVING: Very well, Pastor; speak!

PASTOR MANDERS: Do you remember when, after less than a year of marriage, you stood at the brink of an abyss? Deserted your house and home? Fled from your husband? Yes, Mrs Alving—fled, fled and refused to go back to him, no matter how he begged and pleaded with you?

MRS ALVING: Have you forgotten how infinitely miserable I was that first year?

PASTOR MANDERS: It is just the mark of a rebellious spirit that it craves happiness in this life. What right do we mortals have to happiness? No, we should do our duty, ma'am! And your duty was to keep hold of the man you had chosen, and with whom you were tied in a holy bond.

MRS ALVING: You know the life Alving was leading—

PASTOR MANDERS: I know the rumors about him; and I'd be the last to condone the habits of his youth, if the rumors were true. But a wife is not appointed to be her husband's judge. It was your duty to bear with humility the cross which a Higher Will had, in its wisdom, laid upon you. But instead you throw off the cross in rebellion, desert the stumbling man you should have supported, go and risk your good name and reputation, and—nearly succeed in ruining other people's reputation into the bargain.

MRS ALVING: Other people's? One other person's, don't you mean?

PASTOR MANDERS: It was incredibly reckless of you to seek refuge with me.

MRS ALVING: With our priest? With our intimate friend?

PASTOR MANDERS: Just for that reason. Well, you should thank the Lord God I possessed the necessary strength—that I turned you away from your hysterical plans and that it was vouchsafed me to lead you back to the path of duty and home to your lawful husband.

MRS ALVING: Yes, Pastor Manders, that was certainly your work.

PASTOR MANDERS: I was only a poor instrument in a Higher Hand. And hasn't it grown to be a blessing to you, all the days of your life, that I helped you to bend to duty and obedience? Didn't everything go as I predicted? Didn't Alving turn his back on his straying ways, as a man ought to do? Didn't he live with you from then on, lovingly and purely, all his days? Didn't he become this region's benefactor, and didn't he, in this way, lift you up with him, so that you gradually became his collaborator in all his undertakings? And an able collaborator, too—oh, I know, Mrs Alving, I grant you that. But now I come to the next great misstep of your life.

MRS ALVING: What do you mean?

PASTOR MANDERS: Just as you once disowned a wife's duty, so you have since disowned a mother's.

MRS ALVING: Ah—!

PASTOR MANDERS: You've been ruled all your days by a misbegotten, willful spirit. All you've been drawn to is the insubordinate and the lawless. You've never known how to endure any bond. Everything that has weighed on you in life you've cast away without care or conscience, like a burden you can take or leave at will. It no longer pleased you to be a wife, and you left your husband. You found it inconvenient to be a mother, and you sent your child out to strangers.

MRS ALVING: Yes, that is true. I did that.

PASTOR MANDERS: And now you are a stranger to him.

MRS ALVING: No, no; I am not!

PASTOR MANDERS: You are; you must be. And what kind of son has returned to you? Consider well, Mrs Alving. You sinned greatly against your husband—that you acknowledge by building his memorial. Acknowledge, too, your sin against your son; there may still be time to lead him back from the paths of error. Turn back yourself, and save what may still be saved in him. For in truth, Mrs Alving, as a mother you bear a burden of guilt. I have thought it my duty to say this to you.

(Silence)

MRS ALVING: *(Slowly and carefully)* Now you have spoken, Pastor; tomorrow you'll speak publicly in my husband's memory. I won't speak tomorrow. But now I shall speak a little to you, as you have spoken to me.

PASTOR MANDERS: Naturally; you want to make excuses for your conduct—

MRS ALVING: No. I will only tell a story.

PASTOR MANDERS: Well—?

MRS ALVING: Everything you've said about my husband and me and our life after you brought me back to the path of duty, as you called it, about all that you know nothing firsthand. From that moment, you—our constant companion—never set foot in our house again.

PASTOR MANDERS: You and your husband moved away from town.

MRS ALVING: Yes; and in my husband's lifetime you never came to see us. It was business that forced you to visit me when you agreed to make the arrangements for the Orphanage.

PASTOR MANDERS: *(Softly and hesitatingly)* Helena—if that is meant as a reproach, I would beg you to bear in mind—

MRS ALVING: —Your responsibility to your position, yes. And I was a runaway wife. You can never be too careful with such reckless women.

PASTOR MANDERS: Dear—Mrs. Alving, that is an absurdly overstated—

MRS ALVING: Yes, yes, yes, let it be. I'm only trying to say that when you judge my married life you're relying on nothing but public opinion.

PASTOR MANDERS: I admit that; and what then?

MRS ALVING: But now, Manders, now I will tell you the truth. I have sworn to myself that one day you would know it. You alone!

PASTOR MANDERS: And what is the truth?

MRS ALVING: The truth is that my husband died as depraved as he had lived all his days.

PASTOR MANDERS: *(Feeling for a chair)* What are you saying?

MRS ALVING: After nineteen years of marriage, as depraved—in his lusts at any rate—as he was before you married us.

PASTOR MANDERS: His wildness, when he was young— you call a depraved life!

MRS ALVING: Our doctor used the expression.

PASTOR MANDERS: I don't understand.

MRS ALVING: You don't need to.

PASTOR MANDERS: I am stunned. Your whole marriage—all those years living with your husband were nothing but the abyss, covered up.

MRS ALVING: Neither more nor less. Now you know.

PASTOR MANDERS: This is—it's inconceivable. I can't grasp it! Can't take it in! How was it possible—? How could such a thing be kept secret?

MRS ALVING: That's been my unceasing struggle, day after day. When we had Osvald, I thought Alving seemed to get a little better. But it didn't last. And then I had to fight twice as hard, fight to the death so that no one would learn what kind of man my child had for a father. And you know the way Alving could win people's hearts. No one could ever think anything but good of him. He was one of those people whose life doesn't eat away at their reputation. But then, Manders—you should know this too—then came the most repulsive thing of all.

PASTOR MANDERS: More repulsive than—

MRS ALVING: I'd gone on bearing with him, though I knew very well what was going on in secret away from home. But when the scandal came inside our own four walls—

PASTOR MANDERS: What are you saying! Here!

MRS ALVING: Yes, here in our home. There (*Pointing to the first door on the right*) in the dining room I first got wind of it. I had something to do in there, and the door was standing ajar. I heard our housemaid come up from the garden to water the flowers.

PASTOR MANDERS: Well—?

MRS ALVING: A little later I heard Alving come in. I heard him say something softly to her. And then I heard— *(With a short laugh)* Oh, it still sounds in my ears, so hateful and so ludicrous—I heard my own serving girl whisper: Let me go, Captain! Leave me alone!

PASTOR MANDERS: It was thoughtless and impulsive. But it was a moment's impulse, nothing more, Mrs Alving. Believe me.

MRS ALVING: I soon found out what to believe. The Captain had his way with the girl—and the affair had consequences, Pastor Manders.

PASTOR MANDERS: And all that in this house! In this house!

MRS ALVING: I have borne much in this house. To keep him home at night, I had to keep him company in his secret binges up in his room. I had to sit with him, drink with him, listen to his mindless obscenities, had to fight to drag him into bed—

PASTOR MANDERS: *(Moved)* That you could bear all that.

MRS ALVING: I had my little boy to bear it for. But when the final insult came; when my own serving girl - that's when I swore to myself: I'm putting an end to this! So I took control of the house—total control—over him and everything else. Because now I had a weapon against him, you see; he didn't dare breathe a word. That was when I sent Oswald away. He was going on seven years old, and beginning to notice things and ask questions, the way children do. I couldn't bear it, Manders. I felt the boy would be poisoned by breathing the air in this polluted home. That's why I sent him away. Now you can judge why he never set foot in his home as long as his father lived. No one knows what that cost me.

PASTOR MANDERS: You truly have had a life of trial.

MRS ALVING: I could never have held up if I hadn't had my work. Because I can say I have worked! All the additions to the estate, all the improvements, the useful gadgets Alving was so praised for introducing—do you believe he had the energy for things like that? He lay on the sofa all day, reading old government yearbooks! No; and I'll tell you this, too: the times he was lucid, I was the one who drove him on; and when he started in again, drinking, weeping, feeling sorry for himself, I was the one who had to drag the whole load.

PASTOR MANDERS: And over this man you raise a memorial.

MRS ALVING: There you see the power of a bad conscience.

PASTOR MANDERS: A bad—? What do you mean?

MRS ALVING: I've always felt it would be impossible to keep the truth from coming out. So the Orphanage was meant to smother all the rumors and dispel any doubts.

PASTOR MANDERS: You certainly haven't missed your mark there, Mrs Alving.

MRS ALVING: And I had one more reason. I didn't want my Oswald to inherit anything whatsoever from his father.

PASTOR MANDERS: So it's Alving's fortune that—?

MRS ALVING: Yes. The sums I have spent on the Orphanage, year after year, make up the amount—I have reckoned it exactly—the amount that made Lieutenant Alving such a good catch.

PASTOR MANDERS: I understand—

MRS ALVING: It was my purchase price. I don't want that money to pass into Oswald's hands. Whatever my son gets he will get from me.

(OSWALD *comes through the second door on the right; he has taken off his hat and overcoat in the hall.*)

MRS ALVING: *(Going to him)* Are you back? My dear, my boy!

OSWALD: Yes; what can a man do in this everlasting rain? But I hear we'll eat soon. That's excellent.

REGINA: *(With a package, from the dining room)* A package has come for you, ma'am.

(REGINA *hands it to* MRS ALVING.)

MRS ALVING: *(With a look at* PASTOR MANDERS*)* The music for the dedication tomorrow, I expect.

PASTOR MANDERS: Hm—

REGINA: And luncheon is served.

MRS ALVING: Good; we'll come in a bit; I'll just— *(She starts opening the package.)*

REGINA: *(To* OSWALD*)* Would you like red or white wine, Mister Alving?

OSWALD: Both, please, Miss Engstrand.

REGINA: *Bien*—very well, Mister Alving. *(She goes into the dining room.)*

OSWALD: I might as well help with the corks— *(He likewise goes into the dining room, the door of which swings half open after him.)*

MRS ALVING: *(Having opened the package)* Yes, I thought so; it's the music for the dedication, Pastor Manders.

PASTOR MANDERS: How can I give my speech tomorrow—!

MRS ALVING: Oh, you'll find a way.

PASTOR MANDERS: *(Softly, so as not to be heard in the dining room)* Yes, we mustn't cause a scandal.

MRS ALVING: *(Low but firm)* No. But then this long, hateful farce will be over. From the day after tomorrow I shall act in every way as though the dead had never lived in this house. There will be no one here but my boy and his mother.

(From the dining room, the noise of a chair overturning.)

REGINA: *(Whispering sharply)* Oswald! What's wrong with you? Let me go!

MRS ALVING: *(Starting, terrified)* Ah—!

(MRS ALVING stares wildly towards the half-open door. OSWALD is laughing and humming. A bottle opens with a pop.)

PASTOR MANDERS: *(Agitated)* What's the matter! What is it, Mrs Alving?

MRS ALVING: *(Hoarsely)* Ghosts. The pair from the greenhouse—risen again.

PASTOR MANDERS: What are you saying! Regina—? Is she—?

MRS ALVING: Yes. Come. Not a word—!

(MRS ALVING seizes PASTOR MANDERS by the arm and walks unsteadily towards the dining room.)

END OF ACT ONE

ACT TWO

(The same room. The mist still lies heavy over the landscape.)

(PASTOR MANDERS and MRS ALVING enter from the dining room.)

MRS ALVING: *(Turning to the dining room)* Aren't you coming, Oswald?

OSWALD: *(Off)* No, thanks; I think I'll go out for a while.

MRS ALVING: Yes, do that; it looks a little sunnier now. *(Shutting the dining-room door and going to the hall door and calling)* Regina!

REGINA: *(Off)* Yes, ma'am?

MRS ALVING: Go down to the laundry and help with the garlands.

REGINA: Yes, ma'am.

(MRS ALVING makes sure that REGINA is going, then shuts the door.)

PASTOR MANDERS: You're sure he can't hear us in there?

MRS ALVING: Not with the door shut. Besides, he's going out.

PASTOR MANDERS: I'm still so upset. I don't know how I got down a bite of lunch.

MRS ALVING: *(Controlling her nervousness, walking up and down)* Neither do I. But what's to be done?

PASTOR MANDERS: Yes, what is to be done? I am completely at a loss. I have no experience in such matters.

MRS ALVING: I'm sure no harm has been done yet.

PASTOR MANDERS: No, heaven forbid! But his behavior is inappropriate nonetheless.

MRS ALVING: It's only a whim of Oswald's; you can be sure of that.

PASTOR MANDERS: Yes, as I say, I'm not used to this sort of thing; but still I am positive—

MRS ALVING: Out of the house she goes. At once. That's plain as day—

PASTOR MANDERS: Yes, that's understood.

MRS ALVING: But where to? It wouldn't be right to—

PASTOR MANDERS: Where to? Home to her father, naturally.

MRS ALVING: To whom, did you say?

PASTOR MANDERS: To her—no, but of course Engstrand isn't—but good God, ma'am, how can this be? You just have to be mistaken, that's all.

MRS ALVING: I'm not mistaken, sad to say. Johanna confessed everything to me; and Alving couldn't deny it. So there was nothing to do but keep the affair quiet.

PASTOR MANDERS: No, that was the only thing to do.

MRS ALVING: The girl left our service right away, and got a reasonably generous sum to keep quiet. The rest she took care of herself when she got to town. She renewed an old acquaintance with Engstrand, gave him a hint, I suppose, of how much money she had, and told him some fairy tale about a foreigner who'd been here in a pleasure boat that summer. So she and

Engstrand married in haste. Well, you married them
yourself.

PASTOR MANDERS: But how can I make sense of—?
I remember clearly, Engstrand coming to arrange
about the marriage. He was so contrite, and blamed
himself, bitterly, that he and his fiancée had been so
irresponsible.

MRS ALVING: Well, of course he had to take the blame.

PASTOR MANDERS: But the insincerity of the man! And
with me! I would absolutely not have believed it of
Jacob Engstrand. Well, I am going to give him a serious
talking to; he'd better be ready for that. And the
immorality of such a marriage! For the money—! How
much did the girl get her hands on?

MRS ALVING: It was three hundred crowns.

PASTOR MANDERS: Yes, think of it—three hundred
crowns, to marry a fallen woman!

MRS ALVING: What do you say to me, then, who
married a fallen man?

PASTOR MANDERS: But God save us—what are you
saying? A fallen man!

MRS ALVING: Maybe you think Alving was any more
pure, when we went to the altar, than Johanna was
when Engstrand married her?

PASTOR MANDERS: Well, but that is so different—night
and day—

MRS ALVING: Not so very different in the end. There
was certainly a big difference in price—between three
hundred crowns and a whole fortune.

PASTOR MANDERS: How can you compare such utterly
different things. You were acting on the wishes of your
heart and of your family.

MRS ALVING: *(Not looking at him)* I thought you understood where what you call my heart had been lost at that time.

PASTOR MANDERS: *(Distant)* Had I understood any such thing, I would not have become a daily guest in your husband's home.

MRS ALVING: Well, in any case, my own wishes were never a consideration.

PASTOR MANDERS: Well then, those closest to you, as we are directed, your mother and your aunts.

MRS ALVING: Yes, it's true. The three of them added it up for me. It's unbelievable, how clearly they proved that it would be pure stupidity to turn down such an offer. If Mother could only look up now and see what all that magnificence has come to.

PASTOR MANDERS: No one can be responsible for the outcome. In any case the fact remains, your marriage was made in complete conformity with law and order.

MRS ALVING: *(Going to the window)* Yes, law and order! I often think they're behind all the miseries in the world.

PASTOR MANDERS: Mrs Alving, now you're committing a sin.

MRS ALVING: Well, maybe so. But I won't be bound by those concerns anymore. I can't! I have to work my way to freedom.

PASTOR MANDERS: What do you mean?

MRS ALVING: *(Tapping at the windowpanes)* I never should have concealed the facts of Alving's life. But at the time I didn't dare do anything else—not even for my own sake. I was such a coward.

PASTOR MANDERS: A coward?

MRS ALVING: If people had found out, they'd have said: poor man, it makes sense that he goes astray, him with a wife who ran away from him.

PASTOR MANDERS: But there might be some truth to that.

MRS ALVING: *(Looking steadily at him)* If I were what I should be, I would take Oswald aside and say: listen, my boy, your father was a decadent man—

PASTOR MANDERS: But merciful God—

MRS ALVING: —and then I would tell him all that I've told you—word for word.

PASTOR MANDERS: I find this almost revolting, Madam.

MRS ALVING: Yes, I know. I know it well! I'm revolted at myself, now that I think of it. *(Going from the window)* What a coward I am.

PASTOR MANDERS: And you call it cowardice to do your plain duty and obligation. Have you forgotten that a child should love and honor his father and his mother?

MRS ALVING: Let's not talk in such general terms. Let's ask: should Oswald love and honor Chamberlain Alving?

PASTOR MANDERS: Isn't there a voice in your mother's heart that forbids you to destroy your son's ideals?

MRS ALVING: Yes, but the truth?

PASTOR MANDERS: Yes, but ideals?

MRS ALVING: Oh, —ideals, ideals! If only I weren't the coward I am!

PASTOR MANDERS: Don't throw away ideals, ma'am— they take a cruel revenge. Look at Oswald. Oswald doesn't have many ideals, I'm afraid. But as far as I can judge, his father remains for him a kind of ideal.

MRS ALVING: That's true.

PASTOR MANDERS: And this image of him you've guarded and nourished yourself through your letters.

MRS ALVING: Yes; I was so dutiful and considerate that I lied to my child year in and year out. Oh, what a coward—what a coward I've been!

PASTOR MANDERS: You have built up a happy illusion in your son, Mrs Alving—you mustn't underestimate that.

MRS ALVING: Hm; who knows whether it's done any good at all. But in any case I won't hear of anyone taking advantage of Regina. He mustn't go and get that poor girl into trouble.

PASTOR MANDERS: No, good God, that would be horrible!

MRS ALVING: If I knew that he was serious and that it would make him happy—

PASTOR MANDERS: How? What then?

MRS ALVING: But it couldn't be, I'm afraid; Regina isn't the type.

PASTOR MANDERS: What do you mean?

MRS ALVING: If I weren't the miserable coward I am, I would say to him: marry her, set yourselves up however you want; just don't be dishonest.

PASTOR MANDERS: But merciful God—! A legal marriage, even! Something so appalling—! Something so unheard of—!

MRS ALVING: Unheard of? Honestly, hand on your heart, Pastor Manders; don't you think that out here in the country there are plenty of married couples who are just as closely related?

PASTOR MANDERS: I have no idea what you're talking about.

MRS ALVING: Oh, yes you do.

PASTOR MANDERS: Indeed, you're thinking of cases where it's possible that—. Yes, I'm afraid family life is not always as pure as it should be. But the kind of thing you're referring to, we can never know—in any case not with certainty. Here, on the other hand—; that you, a mother, would be willing to allow your—!

MRS ALVING: But I won't. I couldn't allow it for anything in the world; that's just what I mean.

PASTOR MANDERS: No, because you are a coward, as you put it. So if you weren't a coward—! God my Maker—what an outrageous relationship!

MRS ALVING: Well, besides, we all descend from that sort of relationship, so they say. And who arranged things this way here in the world, Pastor Manders?

PASTOR MANDERS: I won't discuss that sort of question with you, ma'am; you are far from the right frame of mind. But that you dare to call it cowardly of you—!

MRS ALVING: Now you have to hear how I mean that. I'm fearful and timid because sitting inside me are all these ghosts I can never get rid of.

PASTOR MANDERS: What did you call it?

MRS ALVING: Ghosts. When I heard Regina and Oswald in there, it was as if I saw ghosts in front of me. But I almost believe we are all of us ghosts, Pastor Manders. It's not only what we inherit from our father and mother that lives again in us. It's all kinds of old, dead ideas and old, dead beliefs and so on. They aren't alive inside us; but they're there all the same and we can not get rid of them. I pick up a newspaper and I see the ghosts creeping between the lines. There must be ghosts all over this country. As many as the grains of sand, I think. Here we are, so wretchedly afraid of the light, every one.

PASTOR MANDERS: Aha,—so there we have the profits of your reading. Fine fruits, truly! This repulsive, rebellious, freethinking writing!

MRS ALVING: You're mistaken, dear Pastor. The one who first got me thinking was you; it's all thanks to you.

PASTOR MANDERS: Me!

MRS ALVING: Yes, when you forced me to give in to what you called duty and obligation; when you praised as right and proper all that my soul revolted at as loathsome. That was when I began to look at your teachings stitch by stitch. I only wanted to pick at a single knot; but when I'd gotten that loose, it all unraveled. And I saw how shoddy it was.

PASTOR MANDERS: *(Softly, with emotion)* Was that all that was gained by my life's hardest struggle?

MRS ALVING: Call it instead your most pitiful defeat.

PASTOR MANDERS: It was my life's greatest victory, Helena; victory over myself.

MRS ALVING: It was a crime against us both.

PASTOR MANDERS: When I begged you, saying: woman, go home to your lawful husband, when you came to me lost and calling: here I am; take me! Was that a crime?

MRS ALVING: Yes, I think it was.

PASTOR MANDERS: We two do not understand each other.

MRS ALVING: Not anymore, it seems.

PASTOR MANDERS: Never—never in my most secret thoughts have I ever seen you as anything but another man's wife.

MRS ALVING: You believe that?

PASTOR MANDERS: Helena—

MRS ALVING: How easily we lose even the memory of our selves.

PASTOR MANDERS: I am the same as I always was.

MRS ALVING: (*Moving*) Yes, yes, yes—let's not talk about the old days anymore. Now you're up to your ears in commissions and committees; and I stay on here and fight the ghosts, inside me and out.

PASTOR MANDERS: At least I can help you get the better of the ones outside you. After all I've been horrified to hear from you today, I cannot in good conscience allow a young defenseless girl to stay in your house.

MRS ALVING: Don't you think it would be best if we could get her provided for? I mean—by a good marriage.

PASTOR MANDERS: Undoubtedly. I think it would be desirable for her in every respect. Regina is now at the age when—well, I don't know much about these things, but—

MRS ALVING: Regina developed early.

PASTOR MANDERS: Yes, didn't she, though? It seems to me that she was remarkably well developed, in the physical respect, when I prepared her for confirmation. But for the moment anyway she ought to be at home, under her father's eye—no, but Engstrand isn't—That he—that *he* could conceal the truth from me!

(*A knock at the hallway door.*)

MRS ALVING: Who can that be? Come in!

ENGSTRAND: *(In his Sunday clothes, in the doorway)*
I humbly beg your pardon, but—

PASTOR MANDERS: Aha! Hm—

MRS ALVING: Is that you, Engstrand?

ENGSTRAND: —none of the serving girls was around, so
I took the liberty of knocking.

MRS ALVING: Yes, yes indeed. Come in. You want to
speak with me about something?

ENGSTRAND: *(Coming in)* No, thank you all the same. It
was with the Pastor I wanted a bit of a word.

PASTOR MANDERS: *(Walking up and down)*
Hm; well then? You want to speak with me? Do you?

ENGSTRAND: Yes, I'd like so much to—

PASTOR MANDERS: *(Stopping in front of him)* Indeed;
may I ask, what it is you want?

ENGSTRAND: What it was, Pastor, we're getting the last
of our pay. Many thanks, ma'am—And now we're
finished with everything; so I thought it would be
right and proper if we, who have worked together so
wholeheartedly all this time—I thought we should end
with a little prayer meeting tonight.

PASTOR MANDERS: A prayer meeting? Down at the
Orphanage?

ENGSTRAND: Maybe the Pastor doesn't think it's
proper, so—

PASTOR MANDERS: Of course I think so, but—hm—

ENGSTRAND: I've been holding little prayer meetings
down there in the evenings myself—

MRS ALVING: You have?

ENGSTRAND: Yes, now and then; just a little edification, so to speak. But I'm just a poor, common man and don't really have the gift, God help me—so I thought that since Pastor Manders happened to be here, then—

PASTOR MANDERS: Well, you see, Engstrand, first I must ask you a question. Are you in the proper mood for such a gathering? Do you feel your conscience free and at ease?

ENGSTRAND: Oh God help us, we'd better not talk about conscience, Pastor.

PASTOR MANDERS: Well, that is just what we shall speak of. What do you have to say?

ENGSTRAND: Well, conscience—it can be nasty, sometimes.

PASTOR MANDERS: Well, you admit that anyway. But then will you tell me unreservedly—what is your relationship with Regina?

MRS ALVING: *(Quickly)* Pastor Manders!

PASTOR MANDERS: *(Reassuringly)* Allow me—

ENGSTRAND: With Regina! Lord, you gave me a scare! *(Looking at* MRS ALVING*)* There's nothing wrong with Regina, is there?

PASTOR MANDERS: So we hope. But I mean it, how are you and Regina related? You do pass for her father. Well?

ENGSTRAND: *(Uncertain)* Well—hm—the Pastor knows all about me and my blessed Johanna.

PASTOR MANDERS: No more distorting the truth. Your late wife informed Mrs Alving of the true situation before she left her service.

ENGSTRAND: Well then, *she* can—! Did she, though?

PASTOR MANDERS: So you are unmasked, Engstrand.

ENGSTRAND: And she, who swore and gave her sacred oath that—

PASTOR MANDERS: Her oath!

ENGSTRAND: Well, she just swore, but so sincerely.

PASTOR MANDERS: And for all these years you have hidden the truth from me. Hidden it from me, who has so unreservedly trusted you in all things.

ENGSTRAND: Yes, I'm afraid I have.

PASTOR MANDERS: Have I deserved this from you, Engstrand? Haven't I always been ready to help you in word and deed, as far as it lay in my power? Answer me! Haven't I?

ENGSTRAND: There's plenty of times it wouldn't have looked so good for me if it weren't for Pastor Manders.

PASTOR MANDERS: And this is how you repay me. Have me enter falsehoods in the parish register and afterward withhold from me for years the information you owed both to me and to the truth. Your conduct has been altogether unforgivable, Engstrand; and from now on it's over between us.

ENGSTRAND: (With a sigh) Well, that's that, I guess.

PASTOR MANDERS: Yes, because how can you possibly justify yourself?

ENGSTRAND: But should she have gone and disgraced herself even more by talking about it? If the Pastor could just imagine, now, that he were in the same condition as poor Johanna—

PASTOR MANDERS: Me!

ENGSTRAND: Lord, Lord, I don't mean exactly the same. But I mean, if the Pastor had anything to be ashamed of in the eyes of the world, as the saying goes. We men-folk shouldn't judge a poor woman too hard, Pastor.

PASTOR MANDERS: But that's not what I'm doing. I'm addressing my reproaches to you.

ENGSTRAND: May I be permitted to ask the Pastor one tiny little question?

PASTOR MANDERS: Well yes, ask.

ENGSTRAND: Isn't it right and proper for a man to raise up the fallen?

PASTOR MANDERS: Yes, of course.

ENGSTRAND: And isn't a man bound to keep his sincere word of honor?

PASTOR MANDERS: Yes, certainly he is, but—

ENGSTRAND: That time when Johanna got in trouble on account of that Englishman—or was he an American? Russian?—anyway, she came down into town. Poor thing, she'd turned me down a time or two; she only had eyes for what was handsome; and I had this disability in my leg. Well, the Pastor well remembers, I had ventured up into a dance-hall where seafaring men were carrying on—drunk and disorderly, as the saying goes. And when I tried to urge them to find their way to a new life—

MRS ALVING: *(At the window)* Hm—

PASTOR MANDERS: I know, Engstrand; the ruffians threw you down the stairs. You've told me about the incident before. You bear your disability with honor.

ENGSTRAND: I don't make myself haughty about it, Pastor. But this is what I wanted to say, that she came and confessed to me with weeping and gnashing of teeth. I must say, Pastor, it hurt me to the heart to hear it.

PASTOR MANDERS: Did it, Engstrand. Indeed; and then?

ENGSTRAND: Well, so I said to her: the American, he's wandering the oceans of the world. And you, Johanna, I said, you have committed a sin and are a fallen creature. But Jacob Engstrand, I said, has two strong legs to stand on—well, I meant that as sort of a metaphor, Pastor.

PASTOR MANDERS: I understand; go on.

ENGSTRAND: Well, so that was how I raised her up and married her honorably, so people wouldn't find out the way she went wild with foreigners.

PASTOR MANDERS: All that you did splendidly. But I cannot approve of your accepting money—

ENGSTRAND: Money? Me? Not a cent.

PASTOR MANDERS: (*Inquiringly to* MRS ALVING) But—?

ENGSTRAND: Oh—wait a minute; now I remember. Johanna probably did have some pennies after all. But I wouldn't have anything to do with it. Ptui, I said, Mammon, that's the wages of sin; that filthy gold— or bills, whatever it was—we'll throw it back in the American's face, I said. But he was off and gone over the wild ocean, Pastor.

PASTOR MANDERS: Was he, my good fellow?

ENGSTRAND: Oh, yes. And so Johanna and I agreed that the money should go to bring up the child; and so it did; and I can account right and proper for every single cent.

PASTOR MANDERS: But this changes things considerably.

ENGSTRAND: That's the way we're related, Pastor. And may I say I've been an honest father to Regina—as far as it was in my power—for I'm a weak man, I'm afraid.

PASTOR MANDERS: Well, well, my dear Engstrand—

ENGSTRAND: But may I say that I brought up the girl and lived lovingly with blessed Johanna, and I ruled my own house, as the Scripture says. But it never entered my head to go to Pastor Manders and make myself haughty about it, that I, even I had done a good deed in the world. No, when a thing like that happens to Jacob Engstrand, he keeps quiet about it. I know it doesn't go that way too often, I'm afraid. When I do come to Pastor Manders, so much of what I have to talk about is wrongdoing and weakness. For I said it before and I'll say it again—consciences can be nasty now and then.

PASTOR MANDERS: Give me your hand, Jacob Engstrand.

ENGSTRAND: Oh, Lord, Pastor—

PASTOR MANDERS: No nonsense. *(Wringing his hand)* So!

ENGSTRAND: If I might humbly beg the Pastor's pardon—

PASTOR MANDERS: You? No, on the contrary; it is I who should beg your pardon—

ENGSTRAND: Oh, God, no.

PASTOR MANDERS: Absolutely. With all my heart. Forgive me, that I could so misjudge you. And I truly wish to prove to you somehow my sincere regret and my goodwill towards you—

ENGSTRAND: Would you do that, Pastor?

PASTOR MANDERS: With the greatest pleasure—

ENGSTRAND: Because there's a chance to do it now. With the honest money I've saved from my pay up here, I'm thinking I might open a sort of sailors' home down in town.

MRS ALVING: You?

ENGSTRAND: It would be a sort of an orphanage, so to speak. Temptations are so manifold for sailors, when they make their way ashore. But in this home of mine, a man could feel as if he were under a father's wing, I thought.

PASTOR MANDERS: What do you say to that, Mrs Alving!

ENGSTRAND: I don't have very much to get started with, God help me; but if I could just get a helping hand, then—

PASTOR MANDERS: All right, we'll take a closer look at this. Your plan appeals to me very much. But now go ahead of me and make everything ready and get the candles lit, so it can be a bit festive. And then we'll have an edifying time together, my dear Engstrand; for now I believe you are in the proper frame of mind.

ENGSTRAND: I think I am, yes. Good bye, ma'am, and thanks for everything; take good care of Regina for me. *(Wiping a tear from his eye)* Blessed Johanna's child— hm, it's a funny thing—it's just like she's grown up right into my heart. Yes, indeed. *(He bows and goes out through the hall.)*

PASTOR MANDERS: Now what do you say about that man, Mrs Alving! That was a very different explanation we had there.

MRS ALVING: It certainly was.

PASTOR MANDERS: You see how exceedingly cautious one has to be in condemning one's fellow men. But it truly is a joy to ascertain that one has been mistaken. Don't you think?

MRS ALVING: I think you are and will always be a big baby, Manders.

PASTOR MANDERS: Me?

MRS ALVING: *(Laying both hands on his shoulders)* And I think I want to put my arms around that neck of yours.

PASTOR MANDERS: *(Stepping back hastily)* No, no, God bless you—what a thing to want—

MRS ALVING: *(With a smile)* Oh, you shouldn't be afraid of me.

PASTOR MANDERS: *(By the table)* You sometimes have such an exaggerated way of expressing yourself. Now first I will gather the documents and put them in my bag. *(Doing so)* So then. Good bye for now. Keep your eyes open when Oswald comes back. I'll look in on you later. *(He takes his hat and goes out through the hall door.)*

(MRS ALVING sighs, looks out the window, straightens up the room a little, and crosses toward the dining room but stops with a gasp in the doorway.)

MRS ALVING: Oswald, are you still at the table!

OSWALD: *(In the dining room)* Just smoking the last of my cigar.

MRS ALVING: I thought you'd gone for a little walk.

OSWALD: In this weather?

(A glass clinks. MRS ALVING leaves the door open and sits down with her knitting on the sofa by the window.)

OSWALD: *(Within)* Was that Pastor Manders who went out just now?

MRS ALVING: Yes, he went down to the Orphanage.

OSWALD: Hm.

(The glass and carafe clink again.)

MRS ALVING: *(With a troubled glance)* Oswald dear, be careful with that liquor. It's strong.

OSWALD: It's good against the damp.

MRS ALVING: Wouldn't you rather come in here with me?

OSWALD: I'm not supposed to smoke in there.

MRS ALVING: You know very well I don't mind a cigar.

OSWALD: All right then, I'll come in. Just one more little drop. So then. *(He comes, with his cigar, into the room and closes the door behind him. A short silence)* Where's the Pastor gone?

MRS ALVING: I told you, he went down to the Orphanage.

OSWALD: Oh yes, that's right.

MRS ALVING: You shouldn't sit so long at the table, Oswald.

OSWALD: *(Holding his cigar behind him)* But it's such a comfort to me, Mother. *(Stroking and patting her)* Imagine—to be home, at my mother's table, in my mother's house, eating my mother's delicious food.

MRS ALVING: My dear, dear boy!

OSWALD: *(Somewhat impatiently, walking and smoking)* And what else can I do with myself here? I can't work—

MRS ALVING: Can't you?

OSWALD: In weather this grey? Not a glimpse of the sun all day long? *(Walking the floor)* Not being able to work, it's—!

MRS ALVING: Maybe it wasn't so wise for you to come home.

OSWALD: Oh, yes, Mother; I had to.

MRS ALVING: Because I would ten times rather do without the pleasure of having you with me than that you should—

OSWALD: *(Standing by the table)* Tell me, Mother—is it really so great a pleasure for you to have me home?

MRS ALVING: Is it a pleasure for me!

OSWALD: *(Crumpling a newspaper)* I would have thought it must be pretty much all the same to you whether I'm here or not.

MRS ALVING: How do you have the heart to say that to your mother, Oswald?

OSWALD: But you've done well enough living without me so far.

MRS ALVING: Yes, I have lived without you—that is true.

(Silence. Twilight slowly begins to fall. OSWALD walks back and forth. He has put down his cigar.)

OSWALD: *(Stopping beside MRS ALVING)* Mother, may I sit on the sofa with you?

MRS ALVING: *(Making room for him)* Yes, come, my dear boy.

OSWALD: *(Sitting down)* I have something to tell you, Mother.

MRS ALVING: *(Tense)* Well?

OSWALD: *(Staring in front of him)* Because I can't bear it anymore.

MRS ALVING: Bear what? What is it?

OSWALD: I couldn't bring myself to write to you about it; and since I've come home—

MRS ALVING: *(Seizing him by the arm)* Oswald, what's the matter!

OSWALD: Yesterday and today I've tried to push the thoughts away—throw them off. But it doesn't work.

MRS ALVING: *(Rising)* Tell me, Oswald!

OSWALD: *(Drawing her down to the sofa again)* Sit still, and I'll try to tell you. I've complained so much about tiredness from my trip—

MRS ALVING: Well? What then?

OSWALD: But that isn't what's the matter with me; not some ordinary tiredness—

MRS ALVING: *(Trying to rise)* You're not sick, Oswald?

OSWALD: *(Drawing her down again)* Sit still, Mother. Just take it calmly. I'm not really sick either; not like what's ordinarily called sick. *(Clasping his hands over his head)* Mother, it's my mind that's broken down—worn out— I'll never be able to work again!

(OSWALD throws himself, with his hands before his face, down into MRS ALVINGS lap and sobs.

MRS ALVING: *(Pale and trembling)* Oswald! Look at me! No, no, it's not true.

OSWALD: *(Looking up with despair in his eyes)* Never work again! Never—never! It's like a living death! Mother, can you imagine anything so horrible?

MRS ALVING: My poor boy! How did this horrible thing happen to you?

OSWALD: *(Sitting upright again)* That's what I can't understand. I've never really led a tempestuous life. Not in any way. You mustn't believe that about me, Mother! I never have.

MRS ALVING: I believe you, Oswald.

OSWALD: And then this happens to me anyway! This horrible disaster!

MRS ALVING: Oh, but you will get better, my dear, blessed boy. It's nothing but overwork. Believe me.

OSWALD: *(Sadly)* That's what I thought too, at first; but it isn't so.

MRS ALVING: Tell me from start to finish.

OSWALD: I will.

MRS ALVING: When did you notice it first?

OSWALD: It was right after I'd been home the last time and got back to Paris again. I began to feel the most violent pains in my head—mostly here in the back of my head. It felt like a tight iron ring was being screwed around my neck and upward.

MRS ALVING: And then?

OSWALD: At first I thought it was nothing but the usual headaches I'd been so plagued with growing up.

MRS ALVING: Yes, yes—

OSWALD: But that wasn't it; I soon realized. I couldn't work anymore. I'd want to begin on a big new picture; but it would feel as if all my powers were failing me; as if I were paralyzed; I couldn't concentrate; the images swam in front of me—whirling around. It's a horrible way to feel! I finally sent for a doctor—and he gave me the answer.

MRS ALVING: What do you mean?

OSWALD: He was one of the first-rate doctors down there. I told him how I was; and he started asking me a lot of questions that I thought had nothing to do with the case; I had no idea what the man was getting at—

MRS ALVING: Well?

OSWALD: Finally he said: since before you were born, there's been something worm-eaten in you—he used that exact expression, *"vermoulu"*.

MRS ALVING: *(Tense)* What did he mean by that?

OSWALD: I didn't understand either, I begged him to explain more plainly. So the old cynic told me— *(Clenching his fist)* Oh—!

MRS ALVING: What did he say?

OSWALD: He said: the sins of the fathers are visited on the sons.

MRS ALVING: *(Rising slowly)* The sins of the fathers—

OSWALD: I nearly hit him in the face—

MRS ALVING: *(Walking across the floor)* The sins of the fathers—

OSWALD: *(Smiling sadly)* Yes, what do you think of that? Of course I told him that was completely out of the question. But do you think he gave in? No, he stuck to it; and it was only when I took out your letters and translated for him all the parts that had to do with father—

MRS ALVING: But then—?

OSWALD: Well, then of course he had to admit he was on the wrong track; and so I learned the truth. The incomprehensible truth! The life I'd led, a young man's life, with my companions, happy—I should have been safer. I caught something somehow. It's my own fault!

MRS ALVING: Oswald! Oh no; don't believe that!

OSWALD: He said there was no other possible explanation. That's what's so horrible. Infected, infested, incurable—my whole life—by my own carelessness. Everything I wanted to do in the world—I can't think about it—I won't be able to think about it. If only I could live my life over again—undo everything I've done!

(OSWALD throws himself face down on the sofa. MRS ALVING wrings her hands and walks in silent struggle to and fro. After a while, he looks up, propped on his elbows.)

OSWALD: If only it were something I'd inherited—something I hadn't caught myself. But this! What a shameful, thoughtless, reckless way to have squandered my happiness, my health, everything in the world—my future, my life—!

MRS ALVING: No, no, my dear, blessed boy; this is impossible! *(Bending over him)* It isn't as desperate as you think.

OSWALD: Oh, you don't know— *(Springing up)* And then, Mother, to cause you all this misery! So many times I've almost wished you didn't care so much about me after all.

MRS ALVING: I, Oswald; my own boy! The only thing I have in the world; the only thing I care about.

OSWALD: *(Seizing both her hands and kissing them)* Yes, I see that. When I'm home, I see it. And it's part of what's hardest for me. But now you know it all. And we won't talk about it any more today. *(Walking across the floor)* Give me something to drink, Mother!

MRS ALVING: Drink? What do you want to drink?

OSWALD: Oh, anything. You have some cold punch in the house.

MRS ALVING: Yes, but my dear Oswald—!

OSWALD: Mother, don't. Be kind, now! I need something to drown all these thoughts that are eating at me. *(Going up into the greenhouse)* And it's so dark here!

*(*MRS ALVING *pulls a bell-rope on the right.)*

OSWALD: And this never-ending rain. Week after week; months. Never a glimpse of sun. The times I've been home, I never remember seeing the sun shine.

MRS ALVING: Oswald—you're thinking of leaving me!

OSWALD: Hm— *(Drawing a heavy breath)* I'm not thinking of anything. I can't think of anything! *(In a low voice)* I'm leaving that alone.

(REGINA *enters from the dining room.*)

REGINA: You rang, ma'am?

MRS ALVING: Yes, let's get the lamp in.

REGINA: Right away, ma'am. It's already lit. (*She exits.*)

MRS ALVING: (*Going to* OSWALD) Oswald, don't keep anything from me.

OSWALD: I won't, Mother. (*Going to the table*) I think I've told you enough.

(REGINA *brings the lamp and sets it on the table.*)

MRS ALVING: Listen, Regina, would you bring us a split of champagne.

REGINA: Yes, ma'am. (*She goes out again.*)

OSWALD: (*Touching* MRS ALVING *on the head*) That's the way. I knew my mother wouldn't let her boy go thirsty.

MRS ALVING: My poor, dear Oswald; how could I deny you anything now?

OSWALD: Is that true, Mother? You mean it?

MRS ALVING: How? What?

OSWALD: That you couldn't deny me anything?

MRS ALVING: My dear Oswald—

OSWALD: Hush!

(REGINA *brings in a tray with a split of champagne and two glasses, which she sets on the table.*)

REGINA: Shall I open—?

OSWALD: No thanks, I'll do it myself.

(REGINA *goes out again.*)

MRS ALVING: (*Sitting by the table*) What was it you meant—I mustn't deny you?

OSWALD: *(Busy opening the bottle)* First a glass—or two. *(The cork pops; he pours a glass and starts to pour another.)*

MRS ALVING: *(Holding her hand over it)* Thanks—not for me.

OSWALD: More for me then! *(He empties the glass, fills it, and empties it again; then he sits down by the table.)*

MRS ALVING: *(Expectantly)* Well?

OSWALD: *(Without looking at her)* Listen—you and Pastor Manders seemed so strange—um, quiet, at lunch.

MRS ALVING: Did you notice that?

OSWALD: Yes. Um— *(After a short silence)* Tell me— what do you think of Regina?

MRS ALVING: What do I think?

OSWALD: Isn't she beautiful?

MRS ALVING: Dear Oswald, you don't know her as well as I do—

OSWALD: Well?

MRS ALVING: I'm afraid Regina was kept at home too long. I should have brought her here sooner.

OSWALD: *(Filling his glass)* Yes, but doesn't she look beautiful, Mother?

MRS ALVING: Regina has a great many faults—

OSWALD: Oh, what does that matter? *(He drinks again.)*

MRS ALVING: But I'm fond of her anyway; and I am responsible for her. I wouldn't for all the world have any harm come to her.

OSWALD: *(Springing up)* Mother, Regina's my only salvation!

MRS ALVING: *(Rising)* What do you mean?

OSWALD: I can't go on bearing all this anguish alone.

MRS ALVING: Don't you have your mother to bear it with you?

OSWALD: That's what I thought; that's why I came home to you. But it won't work. I see it; it won't work. I can't spend my life out here!

MRS ALVING: Oswald!

OSWALD: I have to live another way, Mother. That's why I have to leave you. I don't want you to see this.

MRS ALVING: My miserable boy! Oh, but, Oswald, as long as you're so sick—

OSWALD: If it were only the sickness, I'd stay with you, Mother. You're my best friend in the world.

MRS ALVING: Yes, that's true, Oswald, isn't it!

OSWALD: (*Drifting restlessly*) But it's all the torment, the regrets, eating away—and then the great killing fear. This horrible fear!

MRS ALVING: (*Following him*) Fear? What fear? What do you mean?

OSWALD: Don't ask me any more. I don't know. I can't describe it for you.

(MRS ALVING *goes over to the right and pulls the bell-cord.*)

OSWALD: What do you want?

MRS ALVING: I want my boy to be happy, that's what I want. He will not go on brooding.

(*To* REGINA, *who comes in the door*)

MRS ALVING: More champagne. A whole bottle.

(REGINA *goes.*)

OSWALD: Mother!

MRS ALVING: Don't you think we know how to live out here in the country?

OSWALD: Isn't she beautiful to look at? The way she's built! And healthy to the core.

MRS ALVING: *(Sitting at the table)* Sit, Oswald, and let's talk calmly together.

OSWALD: *(Sitting)* You don't know, Mother, I have a wrong to make good with Regina.

MRS ALVING: You!

OSWALD: Or a little thoughtlessness—however you want to call it. Quite innocent otherwise. The last time I was home—

MRS ALVING: Yes?

OSWALD: —she asked me so often about Paris, and I told her one thing and another. So as I remember one day I happened to say: wouldn't you like to go there yourself?

MRS ALVING: Well?

OSWALD: I saw she was blushing very red, and then she said: yes, of course, I would love to. Well well, I said, maybe it could be arranged—or some such thing.

MRS ALVING: Oh yes?

OSWALD: Naturally I'd forgotten all about it; but the day before yesterday when I happened to ask her if she was glad that I'd be home for so long—

MRS ALVING: Yes?

OSWALD: —she gave me the funniest look and asked: but what about my trip to Paris?

MRS ALVING: Her trip!

OSWALD: Then I got it out of her that she'd taken it seriously, she'd been thinking about me the whole time, she'd set to work learning French—

MRS ALVING: So that was why—

OSWALD: Mother—when I saw that beautiful, sweet, fresh young girl standing in front of me—I'd never really noticed her till then—but now, when she stood there as if she were ready to take me in with open arms—

MRS ALVING: Oswald!

OSWALD: —then it struck me that she could be my salvation; I saw the joy of life in her.

MRS ALVING: *(Starts)* The joy of life—? Can there be salvation in that?

(REGINA enters from the dining room with a champagne bottle.)

REGINA: *(Setting the bottle on the table)* I'm sorry I took so long, but I had to go to the cellar—

OSWALD: And bring another glass.

REGINA: *(Looking at him, surprised)* There's Madam's glass, Mister Alving.

OSWALD: Yes, but bring one for yourself, Regina.

(REGINA looks startled and throws a quick, shy glance at MRS ALVING.)

OSWALD: Well?

REGINA: *(Softly and hesitantly)* Is it your wish, ma'am—?

MRS ALVING: Bring the glass, Regina.

(REGINA goes out to the dining room.)

OSWALD: *(Looking after her)* Have you noticed how she walks? So firm and free.

MRS ALVING: This cannot happen, Oswald!

OSWALD: It's settled. You'll see. There's nothing to discuss.

(REGINA *comes in with an empty glass, which she keeps in her hand.*)

OSWALD: Sit down, Regina.

(REGINA *looks questioningly at* MRS ALVING.)

MRS ALVING: Sit down.

(REGINA *sits on a chair by the dining room door, still keeping the empty glass in her hand.*)

MRS ALVING: Oswald—what were you saying about the joy of life?

OSWALD: Well, the joy of life, Mother—you don't know a lot about it here at home. I never felt it here.

MRS ALVING: Not when you're with me?

OSWALD: Not when I'm here at home. But you don't understand.

MRS ALVING: Well, yes, I think I almost understand it—now.

OSWALD: That—and then the joy of work, too. Well, it's basically the same thing. But no one here knows about that either.

MRS ALVING: You may be right there. Oswald, let me hear more about this.

OSWALD: Well, all I mean is that people here are brought up to believe that work is a curse and a penance, and that life is a woeful thing that we're better off out of, the sooner the better.

MRS ALVING: A vale of tears, yes. And we so earnestly go about making it that.

OSWALD: But people won't listen to that kind of thing down there. No one there really believes those sermons anymore. Down there it can feel like some jubilant happiness just to be in the world. Mother, have you noticed that everything I've painted has turned on the joy of life? Always and forever on the joy of life. Light and sunshine and holiday air—and human faces radiant with pleasure. That's why I'm afraid to be home with you.

MRS ALVING: Afraid? What are you afraid of here with me?

OSWALD: I'm afraid that everything in me that's most alive would turn ugly here.

MRS ALVING: *(Staring at him)* You think that would happen?

OSWALD: I know it would. Live the same life here at home as down there, and it still wouldn't be the same life.

(MRS ALVING, *who has been listening intently, rises, her eyes wide and thoughtful.*)

MRS ALVING: Now I see how it all hangs together.

OSWALD: What do you see?

MRS ALVING: Now I see for the first time. And now I can speak.

OSWALD: *(Rising)* Mother, I don't understand.

REGINA: *(Who has also risen)* Should I go?

MRS ALVING: No, stay here. Now I can speak. Now, my boy, you'll know everything. And then you can decide. Oswald! Regina!

OSWALD: Be quiet. The Pastor—

PASTOR MANDERS: *(Coming in through the hall door)* Well, we have had a heart-warming time down there.

OSWALD: So have we.

PASTOR MANDERS: Engstrand must have help with this sailors' home. Regina must leave with him and be of help to him—

REGINA: No, thank you, Pastor.

PASTOR MANDERS: *(Noticing her for the first time)* What—? Here, and with a glass in your hand?

REGINA: *(Quickly setting down her glass)* Pardon—!

OSWALD: Regina is leaving with me, Pastor.

PASTOR MANDERS: Leaving! With you!

OSWALD: Yes, as my wife—if she wishes it.

PASTOR MANDERS: But merciful God—!

REGINA: I can't help it, Pastor.

OSWALD: Or she'll stay here, if I stay.

REGINA: *(Involuntarily)* Here!

PASTOR MANDERS: Mrs Alving, I am surprised at you.

MRS ALVING: Neither one will happen; because now I can speak out.

PASTOR MANDERS: But you can't do that! No, no, no!

MRS ALVING: Yes, I can and I will. And without causing any ideals to fall.

OSWALD: Mother, what are you hiding from me!

REGINA: *(Listening)* Ma'am! Listen! People are shouting outside. *(She goes up in the greenhouse and looks out.)*

OSWALD: *(At the window on the left)* What's going on? Where is that light coming from?

REGINA: *(Calling out)* The Orphanage is burning!

MRS ALVING: *(At the window)* Burning!

PASTOR MANDERS: Burning? Impossible. I was just down there.

OSWALD: Where's my hat? Oh, never mind—. Father's Orphanage—! *(He runs out through the garden door.)*

MRS ALVING: My shawl, Regina! It's all in flames.

PASTOR MANDERS: Horrible! Mrs Alving, that fire is a judgment on this misguided house!

MRS ALVING: Yes, yes, of course. Come, Regina.

(MRS ALVING and REGINA hurry out the door.)

END OF ACT TWO

ACT THREE

(The room as before. All the doors stand open. The lamp still burns on the table. Dark outside; except for a slight glimmer through the windows in the background.)

(MRS ALVING, with a shawl over her head, stands up in the greenhouse and looks out. REGINA, also with a shawl on, stands a little behind her.)

MRS ALVING: Burned, all of it. Right to the ground.

REGINA: It's still burning in the basement.

MRS ALVING: Why doesn't Oswald come up. There's nothing left to save.

REGINA: Should I go down and take him his hat?

MRS ALVING: He doesn't have his hat even?

REGINA: *(Pointing to the hallway)* No, it's hanging there.

MRS ALVING: Let it hang there. He has to come up now. I'll see to it myself. *(She goes out through the garden door.)*

PASTOR MANDERS: *(Coming from the hallway)* Isn't Mrs Alving here?

REGINA: She went down through the garden just now.

PASTOR MANDERS: This is the most horrible night I have ever spent.

REGINA: Yes, it's a terrible misfortune, isn't it, Pastor?

PASTOR MANDERS: Oh, don't talk about it! I can hardly bear to think of it.

REGINA: But how could it have happened—?

PASTOR MANDERS: Don't ask me, Miss Engstrand! How would I know? It can't be that you too—? Isn't it enough that your father—?

REGINA: What about him?

PASTOR MANDERS: Oh, he's going to drive me out of my mind.

ENGSTRAND: *(Coming through the hallway)* Pastor—!

PASTOR MANDERS: *(Turning around in terror)* Are you after me here, too!

ENGSTRAND: Oh, I have to—God strike me dead—! Oh, Lord! This is so awful, Pastor!

PASTOR MANDERS: *(Walking to and fro)* Oh dear, oh dear!

REGINA: What is it?

ENGSTRAND: Oh, it's all on account of this prayer-meeting, you see. *(Softly)* We've got our pigeon, my girl! *(Aloud)* And that I could be to blame that Pastor Manders will be blamed for such a thing!

PASTOR MANDERS: But I assure you, Engstrand—

ENGSTRAND: But nobody but the Pastor touched the candles down there.

PASTOR MANDERS: *(Stopping)* Yes, so you claim. But I absolutely cannot recall that I had a candle in my hand.

ENGSTRAND: And I saw, plain as day, the Pastor took a candle and snuffed it with his fingers, and flicked the burning bit of wick into the shavings.

PASTOR MANDERS: You saw that?

ENGSTRAND: Yes, indeed, I saw it plainly.

PASTOR MANDERS: This is just what I can't understand. It's never been my habit to put out candles with my fingers.

ENGSTRAND: It did look like an awful dangerous thing to do. But could it really cause all that, Pastor?

PASTOR MANDERS: *(Walking restlessly to and fro)* Oh, don't ask me!

ENGSTRAND: *(Walking with him)* To go and set fire to the whole thing. Lord, Lord, what a misfortune!

PASTOR MANDERS: *(Wiping the sweat from his forehead)* Yes, you may well say that, Engstrand.

ENGSTRAND: And to think that something like this could happen to a benevolent institution, that would have been a blessing to town and country, they say. The newspapers won't be so gentle with the Pastor, I expect.

PASTOR MANDERS: No, that's just what I'm thinking of. It's almost the worst part of the whole thing. All the spiteful attacks and accusations—! Oh, it's too appalling to think about!

MRS ALVING: *(Coming from the garden)* He won't be persuaded to leave the fire.

PASTOR MANDERS: Oh, here you are, ma'am.

MRS ALVING: So you got out of making your speech, Pastor Manders.

PASTOR MANDERS: Oh, I would so gladly have—

MRS ALVING: *(Softly)* It's best that it's gone as it's gone. This Orphanage was not going to be a blessing to anyone.

PASTOR MANDERS: Don't you think so?

MRS ALVING: Do you think so?

PASTOR MANDERS: But it was an exceedingly great misfortune anyway.

MRS ALVING: We'll talk it over once and for all, as a business matter. Are you waiting for the Pastor, Engstrand?

ENGSTRAND: *(At the hall door)* Yes, that's just what I'm doing.

MRS ALVING: Then sit down in the meantime.

ENGSTRAND: Thanks, I'd rather stand.

MRS ALVING: *(To* PASTOR MANDERS*)* I suppose you'll leave on the steamboat?

PASTOR MANDERS: Yes. It goes in an hour.

MRS ALVING: Then be so good as to take all the paperwork back with you. I don't want to hear another word on the subject. I have other things to think about—

PASTOR MANDERS: Mrs Alving—

MRS ALVING: Later I'll send you a power of attorney to settle everything as you please.

PASTOR MANDERS: I'll be glad to take care of it. The foundation's original mission must now be changed altogether, I'm afraid.

MRS ALVING: That's understood.

PASTOR MANDERS: Yes, so I think first of all I'll arrange that the Solvig estate should go to the parish. The land itself can hardly be said to be utterly worthless. It can always be put to another use. And the interest on the endowment I might perhaps apply to the benefit of some other project that may be of use to the town.

MRS ALVING: Absolutely, as you wish. It makes no difference to me.

ENGSTRAND: Think about my sailor's home, Pastor!

PASTOR MANDERS: Well, certainly, you're saying something there. Indeed, that must be carefully considered.

ENGSTRAND: To hell with considering— Oh, Lord!

PASTOR MANDERS: *(With a sigh)* And I'm afraid I don't know how long I will be dealing with these matters. If public opinion doesn't force me to retire. It all depends on the outcome of the inquiry into the fire.

MRS ALVING: What do you mean?

PASTOR MANDERS: And there's no predicting what the outcome will be.

ENGSTRAND: Oh, yes there is. For here stands Jacob Engstrand.

PASTOR MANDERS: Well, yes, but—?

ENGSTRAND: *(Softer)* And Jacob Engstrand is not a man who deserts a noble benefactor in the hour of need, as the saying goes.

PASTOR MANDERS: Well, my dear man—how—?

ENGSTRAND: Jacob Engstrand, he's like a guardian angel come to save you, Pastor!

PASTOR MANDERS: No, no, that I absolutely cannot accept.

ENGSTRAND: Well, that's how it's going to be anyhow. I know somebody who's taken the blame for somebody else before now.

PASTOR MANDERS: Jacob! *(Wringing his hand)* You are a rare person. Indeed, you shall be helped with your sailor's asylum; you can be sure of that.

(ENGSTRAND *tries to thank* PASTOR MANDERS, *but cannot for emotion.*)

PASTOR MANDERS: *(Hanging his traveling-bag on his shoulder)* And so we're off. The two of us will travel together.

ENGSTRAND: *(At the dining room door, softly to Regina)* You come along with me, Miss. You'll live as cozy as the yolk in an egg.

REGINA: *(Tossing her head) Merci!*

(REGINA goes out into the hall and fetches the PASTOR MANDERS's raincoat.)

PASTOR MANDERS: Good-bye, Mrs Alving! And may the spirit of order and lawfulness quickly descend on this house.

MRS ALVING: Farewell, Manders!

(MRS ALVING goes up towards the greenhouse, as she sees OSWALD come in through the garden door.)

ENGSTRAND: *(As he and REGINA help PASTOR MANDERS into his coat)* Farewell, my child. And if anything happens to you, then you know where to find Jacob Engstrand. *(Softly)* Little Harbor Street, hm—! *(To MRS ALVING and OSWALD)* And my home for wayfaring seamen shall be called "Chamberlain Alving's Home". And if I can run it the way I have in mind, may I say it will be worthy of the blessed Chamberlain's name.

PASTOR MANDERS: *(In the doorway)* Hm—hm! Come then, my dear Engstrand. Farewell; farewell!

(ENGSTRAND and PASTOR MANDERS go out through the hall.)

OSWALD: *(Going over to the table)* What home was he talking about?

MRS ALVING: It's a kind of asylum that he and Pastor Manders want to set up.

OSWALD: It will burn up just like this one here.

MRS ALVING: What makes you think that?

OSWALD: Everything will burn. There'll be nothing left in memory of my father. Here I am, too, burning up.

(REGINA *looks steadily at him.*)

MRS ALVING: Oswald! You shouldn't have stayed so long down there, my poor boy.

OSWALD: (*Sitting down by the table*) I think you may be right.

MRS ALVING: Let me dry your face, Oswald; you're very wet.

(MRS ALVING *dries* OSWALD *with her pocket-handkerchief.*)

OSWALD: (*Looking indifferently in front of him*) Thanks, Mother.

MRS ALVING: Aren't you tired, Oswald? Maybe you'd like to sleep?

OSWALD: (*Fearful*) No, no—not sleep! I never sleep; I just lie there. (*Sadly*) That'll come soon enough.

MRS ALVING: (*Looking worriedly at him*) Well, you are certainly sick, though, my blessed boy.

REGINA: (*Tensely*) Is Mister Alving sick?

OSWALD: (*Impatiently*) Then shut all the doors! This killing fear—

MRS ALVING: Shut them, Regina.

(REGINA *shuts them and stays standing by the hallway door.* MRS ALVING *takes off her shawl.*)

MRS ALVING: (*Drawing a chair toward* OSWALD *and sitting with him*) So then; now I want to sit with you—

OSWALD: Yes, do that. And Regina will stay, too. Regina will always be with me. You'll lend me a helping hand, Regina, won't you?

REGINA: I don't understand—

MRS ALVING: A helping hand?

OSWALD: Yes—when it's needed.

MRS ALVING: Oswald, don't you have your mother's hand to help you?

OSWALD: You? *(Smiling)* No, Mother, this helping hand you can't give me. *(Laughing sadly)* You! Ha ha! *(Looking earnestly at her)* You know, you would be the next best one for it. *(Impetuously)* Why are you so formal with me, Regina? Why don't you call me Oswald?

REGINA: *(Softly)* I don't think Madam would like that.

MRS ALVING: You'll have the right to, soon. You sit here with us, too.

(REGINA sits demurely and hesitantly at the other side of the table.)

MRS ALVING: And now, my poor, suffering boy, now I will take the burden from your mind—

OSWALD: You, Mother?

MRS ALVING: —all of what you called the regrets and reproaches, eating away—

OSWALD: You think you can do that?

MRS ALVING: Now I can, Oswald. You spoke before about the joy of life; and it was as if a new light shone for me over everything in my whole life.

OSWALD: *(Shaking his head)* I don't understand any of this.

MRS ALVING: You should have known your father when he was a very young lieutenant. He was full of the joy of life!

OSWALD: Yes, I know.

MRS ALVING: It was like a holiday just to look at him. And the irrepressible strength and vitality he had!

OSWALD: And then—?

MRS ALVING: And then this child, full of the joy of life—for he was like a child then—he had to make his home here in a second-rate town that had no joy to offer him, only pastimes. He had to get along here with no purpose in life; only a title. He didn't have any work he could throw himself into with all his soul; only business. He didn't have a single companion who could feel what the joy of life is; only drunkards and parasites—

OSWALD: Mother—!

MRS ALVING: So what had to happen, did happen.

OSWALD: And what had to happen?

MRS ALVING: You said yourself, earlier this evening, what would happen to you if you stayed at home.

OSWALD: Do you mean to say that Father—?

MRS ALVING: Your poor father never found any outlet for the overpowering joy of life that was in him. Even I couldn't bring any holiday air into his home.

OSWALD: Not even you?

MRS ALVING: They'd taught me some things about duty and so on that I went on believing so long. Everything came out as duties—*my* duties and *his* duties and—I'm afraid I made his home unbearable for your poor father, Oswald.

OSWALD: Why haven't you ever written anything to me about this?

MRS ALVING: I've never seen it before, not in such a way that I could touch on it with you, his son.

OSWALD: And how did you see it then?

MRS ALVING: *(Slowly)* I saw only one thing, that your father was a worm-eaten man before you were born.

OSWALD: *(Choked)* Ah—! *(He rises and goes to the window.)*

MRS ALVING: Then day in and day out I kept thinking one thing, that after all Regina had as much right to be in this house—as much as my own child.

OSWALD: *(Turning quickly)* Regina—!

REGINA: *(Springing up and asking, choked)* Me—?

MRS ALVING: Yes, now you know, both of you.

OSWALD: Regina!

REGINA: *(To herself)* So that's what Mother was like.

MRS ALVING: Your mother was good in many ways, Regina.

REGINA: Yes, but that's what she was like anyway. Yes, I've wondered now and then; but—Well, ma'am, then may I have permission to leave here at once?

MRS ALVING: Do you really want to do that, Regina?

REGINA: Of course I do.

MRS ALVING: Naturally, you do what you want, but—

OSWALD: *(Going toward* REGINA*)* Go away now? You belong here.

REGINA: *Merci*, Mister Alving—well, now I do get to call you Oswald. But it certainly isn't in the way I would have wanted.

MRS ALVING: Regina, I haven't been candid with you—

REGINA: No, sad to say! If I'd known then that Oswald was sick—And now that it can't come to anything serious between us—No, I really can't stay out here in the country and wear myself out for sick people.

OSWALD: Not even for someone so close to you?

REGINA: No, I can't. A poor girl's got to make use of her youth, or she'll be out in the cold before she knows it. And I have the joy of life in me, too, ma'am!

MRS ALVING: Yes, I'm afraid so; but don't just throw yourself away, Regina.

REGINA: Oh, whatever will happen, will happen. Since Oswald takes after his father, I may as well take after my mother, I suppose. May I ask, ma'am, if Pastor Manders knows the truth about me?

MRS ALVING: Pastor Manders knows all about it.

REGINA: *(Getting busy with her shawl)* Then I'd better get to the steamboat as fast as I can. The Pastor is so kind a man to deal with; and I think I have as much right to a bit of that money as he does—that awful carpenter.

MRS ALVING: You are quite welcome to it, Regina.

REGINA: *(Looking at her hard)* Madam could have easily brought me up as a gentleman's daughter; it would have suited me better. *(Tossing her head)* Never mind— it's all the same! *(With a bitter side-glance at the corked bottle)* I may get to drink champagne with the gentry yet.

MRS ALVING: If you're ever in need of a home, Regina, come to me.

REGINA: No, many thanks, ma'am. Pastor Manders, he'll take care of me. And if things really go wrong, I know a house where I have a rightful home.

MRS ALVING: Where is that?

REGINA: In Chamberlain Alving's Home.

MRS ALVING: Regina—I see it now—you're going to destroy yourself.

REGINA: Oh, pfft! *Adieu. (She bows and goes out through the hallway.)*

OSWALD: *(Standing by the window and looking out)* She's gone?

MRS ALVING: Yes.

OSWALD: *(Murmuring to himself)* I think it's all wrong, here.

MRS ALVING: *(Going behind him and laying her hands on his shoulders)* Oswald, my dear boy—has it shaken you very much?

OSWALD: *(Turning to her)* All this about Father, you mean?

MRS ALVING: Yes, about your unhappy father. I'm afraid it might have been too much for you.

OSWALD: How can you think that? Of course it comes as quite a surprise; but after all it's more or less all the same to me.

MRS ALVING: *(Drawing her hands away from him)* All the same! That your father was so tremendously unhappy!

OSWALD: Naturally I can feel sympathy for him, as for any other man, but—

MRS ALVING: No differently! For your own father!

OSWALD: *(Impatiently)* Oh, father, father. I've never known a thing about Father. I don't remember anything about him except that once he made me throw up.

MRS ALVING: This is horrible to think of! Shouldn't a child feel love for his father in any case?

OSWALD: When a son has nothing to thank his father for? Never knew him? Do you really hold onto that old superstition, when you're so enlightened in other ways?

MRS ALVING: And can it be just a superstition—!

OSWALD: Yes, you can see that, Mother. It's one of these ideas that are put into circulation in the world and then—

MRS ALVING: *(Shaken)* Ghosts!

OSWALD: *(Walking across the floor)* Yes, you could certainly call them ghosts.

MRS ALVING: *(Crying out)* Oswald—then you don't love me either!

OSWALD: I know you, in any case—

MRS ALVING: Yes, know me; but that's all!

OSWALD: And I know well how fond you are of me; and for that of course I'm grateful to you. And then you can be so useful to me, now that I'm sick.

MRS ALVING: Yes, can't I, Oswald! Oh, I could almost bless your illness, when it's driven you home to me. For I see well enough; I do not have you; I have to win you.

OSWALD: *(Impatiently)* Yes, all right; those are just a lot of stock phrases now. Try to bear in mind, I'm a sick man, Mother. I can't worry so much about other people; I have enough to do thinking about myself.

MRS ALVING: *(In a low voice)* I shall be easily satisfied and patient.

OSWALD: And cheerful, Mother!

MRS ALVING: Yes, my dear boy, you're right. *(Going to him)* Now have I taken away all the reproaches that were eating away—

OSWALD: Yes, you have. But who's going to take away the fear?

MRS ALVING: The fear?

OSWALD: *(Walking across the floor)* Regina would have done it for one kind word.

MRS ALVING: I don't understand you. What is this about fear—and Regina?

OSWALD: Is it very late at night, Mother?

MRS ALVING: It's early in the morning. *(Looking out through the greenhouse)* Day is beginning to break above the mountains. And the weather is clear, Oswald! In a little while you'll see the sun.

OSWALD: I'm glad of that. Maybe there's plenty for me to be glad of and live for—

MRS ALVING: I should think so!

OSWALD: Even if I can't work, then—

MRS ALVING: Oh, you'll get to work again, very soon, my dear boy. Now that you don't have those gnawing, oppressive thoughts to brood over anymore.

OSWALD: No, it was good that you got rid of those nightmares of mine. And now when I just get over this one— *(Sitting on the sofa)* Now let's talk together, Mother—

MRS ALVING: Yes, let's.

(MRS ALVING pulls an armchair near the sofa and sits close to OSWALD.)

OSWALD: —and meanwhile the sun will rise. Then you'll know. And I won't feel this fear anymore.

MRS ALVING: What do you mean, I'll know?

OSWALD: *(Without listening to her)* Mother, didn't you say earlier this evening that there was nothing in the world you wouldn't do for me, if I asked you?

MRS ALVING: Yes, of course I did!

OSWALD: And you'll stand by that, Mother?

MRS ALVING: You can count on that, my own dear boy. I don't live for anything but you.

OSWALD: All right, then you'll listen. Mother, you have a strong, powerful mind, I know it. You'll stay very calm when you hear.

MRS ALVING: But what is this horrible thing—!

OSWALD: You won't cry. Do you hear? Do you promise me that? You will sit and talk very quietly about it. Promise me, Mother?

MRS ALVING: All right, I promise you; but tell!

OSWALD: Well, then, it's time you know that my tiredness—my not being able to think about work—all that is not the disease itself—

MRS ALVING: What is the disease itself?

OSWALD: The disease I've been given as my birthright, the one— *(Pointing to his forehead and adding very softly)* the one in here.

MRS ALVING: *(Nearly speechless)* Oswald! No—no!

OSWALD: Don't scream. I can't bear it. Yes, it's in here, waiting. It can break out any time, any moment.

MRS ALVING: Oh, how horrible—!

OSWALD: Just be calm now. That's how it stands with me—

MRS ALVING: *(Springing up)* This is not true, Oswald! It is impossible! It can't be!

OSWALD: I had one attack down there. It was over soon. But when I found out what had happened, then the fear came, raging and hounding me, so I left for home, to you, as fast as I could.

MRS ALVING: So this is the fear—!

OSWALD: Yes, because it's so unspeakably disgusting, you see. If it had only been an ordinary deadly disease—I'm not afraid to die; though I'd gladly live as long as I can.

MRS ALVING: Yes, yes, Oswald, you must!

OSWALD: But this is so horribly disgusting. To become like a baby again; to have to be fed, to have to be—It's unspeakable!

MRS ALVING: A child has his mother to nurse him.

OSWALD: *(Springing up)* No, never; that is just what I will not have! I can't bear to think that I might lie there like that for years—get old and grey. And meanwhile you might die before me. *(Sitting in* MRS ALVING's *chair)* Because the doctor said it might not turn out to be deadly right away. He called it a sort of softening of the brain—something like that. *(Smiling sadly)* I think that expression sounds so sweet. I always start to think of cherry-colored velvet—something delicate to stroke.

MRS ALVING: *(Screaming)* Oswald!

OSWALD: *(Springing up again and walking across the floor)* And now you've taken Regina away from me! If only I had her. She would have given me a helping hand.

MRS ALVING: *(Going to him)* What do you mean, my darling boy? Is there any help in the world that I wouldn't give you?

OSWALD: When I came to myself after the attack down there, the doctor told me that when it comes again—and it will come again—there will be no more hope.

MRS ALVING: And he was heartless enough to—

OSWALD: I demanded it from him. I told him I had preparations to make— *(Smiling cunningly)* And I have. *(Taking a little box out of his inside breast pocket)* Mother, do you see this?

MRS ALVING: What is it?

OSWALD: Morphine.

MRS ALVING: *(Staring at him, horrified)* Oswald, my boy?

OSWALD: I've got twelve capsules saved up—

MRS ALVING: *(Grabbing for it)* Give me the box, Oswald!

OSWALD: Not yet, Mother. *(He puts the box back in his pocket.)*

MRS ALVING: I'll never survive this!

OSWALD: You have to survive it. If I'd had Regina here, I'd have told her how it stood with me—and begged her to lend me a helping hand at the end. She'd have helped me; I'm sure of that.

MRS ALVING: Never!

OSWALD: When the horror had come over me and she saw me lying there helpless, like a little new-born baby, helpless, lost, beyond hope—nothing left to save—

MRS ALVING: Never in the world would Regina have done that!

OSWALD: Regina would have done it. Regina was so beautifully light-hearted. She'd soon have gotten tired of nursing someone as sick as me.

MRS ALVING: Then praise God that Regina's not here!

OSWALD: So now you have to be the one who lends me a helping hand, Mother.

MRS ALVING: *(Shrieking aloud)* I!

OSWALD: Who better than you?

MRS ALVING: I! Your mother!

OSWALD: Just so.

MRS ALVING: I, who have given you life!

OSWALD: I didn't ask you for life. And what sort of life have you given me? I won't have it! Take it back!

MRS ALVING: Help! Help! *(She runs out into the hallway.)*

OSWALD: *(After her)* Don't leave me! Where are you going?

MRS ALVING: *(In the hallway)* To get the doctor for you, Oswald! Let me go out!

OSWALD: *(In the same place)* You won't go out. And no one will come in.

(A key turns.)

MRS ALVING: *(Coming in again)* Oswald! Oswald, my child!

OSWALD: *(Following her)* Don't you have a mother's heart for me—when you can see me suffering all this unspeakable fear!

(A moment of stillness. MRS ALVING pulls herself together.)

MRS ALVING: Here is my hand on it.

OSWALD: Will you—?

MRS ALVING: If it is necessary. But it will not be necessary. No, no, it isn't possible!

OSWALD: Yes, let's hope for that. And so let's live together as long as we can. Thanks, Mother.

(OSWALD sits in the armchair that MRS ALVING moved to the sofa. Day is breaking; the lamp is still burning on the table.)

MRS ALVING: *(Nearing him cautiously)* Do you feel calm now?

OSWALD: Yes.

MRS ALVING: *(Bending over him)* It has been a horrible nightmare for you, Oswald. All a nightmare. You can't stand all this excitement. But now you can rest. Home

with your own mother, my blessed boy. Everything
you point to, you shall have it, just like when you were
a little child. So then. Now your attack is over. See
how easily it passed! Oh, I knew it would. And you
see, Oswald, what a lovely day we're going to have?
Brilliant sunshine. Now you can really get to see your
home.

(MRS ALVING *goes to the table and puts out the lamp.*
Sunrise. The glaciers and peaks in the background lie in the
brilliant morning light.)

(OSWALD *sits in the armchair with his back to the*
background, without moving.)

OSWALD: *(Suddenly)* Mother, give me the sun.

MRS ALVING: *(At the table, looking at him, startled)* What
are you saying?

OSWALD: *(Dull and tonelessly)* The sun. The sun.

MRS ALVING: *(Going to him)* Oswald, what's the matter
with you?

(OSWALD *seems to shrivel in the chair; all his muscles go*
slack; his face is expressionless; his eyes gaze out, dull.)

MRS ALVING: *(Trembling in fright)* What is this? *(Crying*
aloud) Oswald! What is the matter with you! *(Throwing*
herself on her knees by him and shaking him) Oswald!
Oswald! Look at me! Don't you know me?

OSWALD: *(Tonelessly as before)* The sun. The sun.

MRS ALVING: *(Springing up in despair, raking her hands*
in her hair and shrieking) I can't bear this! *(Whispering,*
frozen) I can't bear this! Never! *(Suddenly)* Where has he
got them? *(Fumbling swiftly over his chest)* Here! *(Taking*
two steps back and screaming) No; no; no! —Yes! —No,
no!

(MRS ALVING *stands a pair of steps away from* OSWALD, *with her hands entangled in her hair and staring at him in speechless horror.*)

(OSWALD *sits motionless as before.*)

OSWALD: The sun. The sun.

END OF PLAY

www.ingramcontent.com/pod-product-compliance
Lightning Source LLC
Chambersburg PA
CBHW052158090426
42741CB00010B/2317